POLITICAL PLAYS FOR CHILDREN

THE GRIPS THEATER OF BERLIN

POLITICAL PLAYS
FOR
CHILDREN

THE GRIPS THEATER OF BERLIN

edited & translated by

JACK ZIPES

TELOS PRESS • SAINT LOUIS

Acknowledgements

The American versions of all three plays, *Mugnog, Bizzy, Dizzy, Daffy and Arthur*, and *Man oh Man*, have been changed somewhat to correspond to the living conditions in the USA. However, in no way have the basic aims and ideas of the original plays been altered. The attempt has been made to develop them in a way that will be meaningful to American children.

In doing the translations, I was especially aided by Baerbel and Ken Rugg, who have produced these plays and *Trummi kaputt* in California. Not only have they made fine suggestions for adapting the original works, but they have organized one of the better children's theater ensembles, Stone Soup, which has broken new ground in America. In addition to the Ruggs and Stone Soup, I have also benefited from my work with Theatre X and the group The Otters and the Hounds in Milwaukee.

Pamela Bro-Harrison and Barbara Correll made numerous helpful changes in editing the manuscripts. Anne Warren was instrumental in re-arranging the music to correspond to the English texts. Wendy Cooper designed the cover and has given me important advice in all matters pertaining to art. Finally, I want to thank Melchior Schedler, whose critical endeavors in the field of children's theater have been exemplary; Jörg Richard, whose essays and advice have helped me clarify many of my own ideas about emancipatory children's theater; and Volker Ludwig, whose work and support have in effect made this volume possible.

Table of Contents

GRIPS
Toward an Emancipatory Theater for Children

by Jack Zipes

Until the late 1960s there was hardly a word published about children's theater in West Germany. None of the major books on theater in West Germany ever mentioned children's theater, and *Theater heute*, the major drama magazine, published only one article about fairy-tale plays between 1960 and 1969. If one wanted to be malicious, one could argue that the neglect of children's theater is due to the negligent, abusive manner in which children are treated in West Germany. No doubt there is some truth to this statement, as Germans themselves have written tracts about the peculiar manifestations of *Kinderfeindlichkeit* (hostility to children) in the German tradition. But the real reason for the disregard of children's theater is due to the puerile, unimaginative regressive quality of the plays which have socially been trimmed according to the trimming process of repressive education foisted upon German children.

Generally speaking, the dominant influence in German children's theater has been the childish, feudal fairy-tale play which presents a rosy, Disneyland image of a clean-cut world for kids who are cut to be clean. From 1854 (the beginnings of children's theater) through the Wilhelmian era, from the creation of the Weimar Republic in 1919 through the Nazi epoch, from the establishment of the Federal Republic of Germany in 1949 to the present, German children have been given a steady diet of banal, cute plays diluted of reality in order to distract them from their real oppressive surroundings and to keep them unaware of how they might use their wits and initiative to develop their full potentialities and possibly change society. That is, until recently. Until the advent of Grips.

Whether one is pro or contra Grips, no one would dispute the fact that Grips has changed the children's theater scene and that, since 1969, children's theater is being taken more seriously in West Germany. In fact, it could be argued that Grips has become the pacesetter for a new emancipatory children's theater in the entire western world. As Volker Ludwig, the head of Grips theater, has stated: "The purpose of our theater is emancipatory education. We want to show that our conditions are changeable and to help audiences see this. In this way, we hope to show different possibilities and to foster critical thinking. Primarily this means that we want to encourage children to ask questions, to understand that criticism is their undeniable right, to enjoy creative thinking, and to gain pleasure from seeing alternatives and making changes." In other words, this new Berlin children's theater wants to show children how to make full use of their *Grips*. It is difficult to render an exact translation of *Grips*, which is German slang for wit, common sense, and imagination taken together. To have *Grips* implies that you can use your brains to master any situation, which is what Ludwig's theater wants to help children do while, at the same time, demonstrating how much pleasure they can get from using *Grips*.

The concept and practice of emancipatory theater developed by the Grips ensemble has an interesting history which reveals how difficult it has been to overcome the repressive training which children are obliged to experience in West Germany. Both on a personal and general level, the history of the Grips theater shows how New Left artists have undergone and are still undergoing an arduous process of developing their political consciousness and how these essentially "bourgeois" writers, actors, musicians, and technicians have endeavored to reutilize their skills to serve the working classes. Brecht speaks about the *Umfunktionierung* (reutilization) of bourgeois culture necessary to move toward socialism, and by this, he means turning around and using talents developed by bourgeois society to serve the emerging working class so that greater social emancipation might be achieved. In this sense, the history of the Grips theater is one of *Umfunktionierung*.

Strange to say, the "ancient" beginnings of the Grips theater are rooted in a prisoner of war camp. Eckart Hachfeld (the father of Volker Ludwig), whose ancestors were loyal rigid Prussian officers, and who received a strongly conservative education, began writing skits and plays to amuse his fellow German prisoners. After the war, instead of pursuing a career as lawyer, Hachfeld continued to write cabaret sketches and songs which tended to satirize the political conservatism and social conditions in West Germany. It was obvious that the war and the contradictory developments during the postwar period in West Germany had moved Hachfeld to abandon his own conservative politics and to side with the Social Democrats, as the political tone of his cabaret skits clearly indicated. Hachfeld soon made a name for himself as the leading cabaret writer of the postwar period while also writing successful screenplays for various film corporations. In 1952 he became the chief author of the Düsseldorfer Kom(m)ödchen, traditionally known as the most liberal and experimental cabaret in West Germany, where he still works today.

It was in an artistic milieu, so to speak, also influenced strongly by the mother's Moravian Church background, which added a moral fiber to their education, that the three Hachfeld sons were raised: Eckart (Volker Ludwig, b. 1937, who heads Grips today); Rainer (b. 1939, one of the leading caricaturists in West Germany, who also writes children's plays and does all the art work for Grips); Tilman (b. 1942, a progressive Protestant minister in Switzerland). Ludwig began writing sketches and songs while still a high school student. Though his father never encouraged him to follow in his footsteps as it were, his father's work had a great influence on him. In 1954 already, because he was having his first short stories published, Ludwig changed his family name so he would not become confused with his father. During his years at the universities of Berlin and Munich (1957-1961), Ludwig concentrated on studying German literature, but his real interest was still in writing songs, stories, and sketches.

In 1961 he returned to West Berlin, and, as he himself admits, decided to see how much money he could make with his talent. Until 1965, Ludwig wrote hit songs, shows for radio and tv, skits for cabarets, and advertisements. And he virtually rolled in money. There was no doubt that he could "make it," but Ludwig began to have doubts about his commercial work which he no longer enjoyed. He also began to have a guilty conscience because he was not doing anything constructive with his money. In addition, many of his friends, who were gradually becoming engaged in political activities on the Left, were highly critical of his life style and work. So it was out of a guilty conscience, Ludwig maintains, that he founded the Reichskabarett in 1965, which was to become the leading political cabaret in West Berlin, if not in all of West Germany. Ludwig was able to bring together some of the best cabaretists in the country including his father, his brother Rainer, Wolfgang Neuss and such outstanding performers as Dieter Kursawe, Joachim Kemmer, Wolfgang Wiehe, and later Jörg Friedrich, Dietrich Lehmann, Renate Küster, and Ulrich Gressieker, who are still with the Grips ensemble. It was there also that the gifted musician Birger Heymann began working. Though the Reichskabarett displayed a social critical tendency from the beginning, it was not until its famous anti-Vietnam show of 1966 and the active response of politicized students, who attended the cabaret most frequently, that the Reichskabarett moved more and more to the Left. By 1968, with its production of *Der Guerilla lässt grüssen* (*The Guerilla Sends his Regards*), which was conceived in collaboration with the anti-authoritarian wing of SDS centering around Rudi Dutschke, the Reichskabarett became recognized as the number one political cabaret of the New Left, both on an artistic and an intellectual level.

While the Reichskabarett performed political skits for adults during the evenings, in June of 1966 it began to produce plays for children during the day. The first show was written by two of the actors and was entitled *The Devil with the Three Golden Hairs*, a clever adaptation of a Grimms fairy tale. Next came another stock-in-trade play, *Renard the Fox*, which did not satisfy the members of the Reichskabarett since it repeated most of the banal mistakes of the insipid fairy-tale plays. Actress Sigrid Hackenberg, who was directing the children's plays, encouraged members of the ensemble to write their own original works, more critical of the social realities. Horst Jüssen responded with five new plays: *Kaspar und der Löwe Poldi I und II* (*Kaspar and the Lion Poldi I and II*, 1967-68), *Der Floh ist weg* (*The Flea Is Away*, 1967), *Weihnachten in Petersilien* (*Christmas in Petersilien*, 1968), *Im Wilmersdorf ist heute wilder Westen* (*There's a Wild West Show in Wilmersdorf Today*, 1969). In spite of Hackenberg's inventive directing and Horst A. Hass' extraordinary music, none of these plays really broke with the tradition of fairy tale or artificial Donald Duck routines of children's plays. The last one, which was intended to be a parody of American westerns, caused an argument among members of the ensemble. Ludwig took the position that the play was geared more toward adults than children and contained too many slick elements of tv shows. Hackenberg was of another opinion, and she left the Reichskabarett along with most of the performers of the children's theater in the spring of 1969.

In the meantime, Ludwig and his brother Rainer Hachfeld had already begun writing plays for children which showed signs of moving in a totally new direction. *Die Reise nach Pitschepatsch* (*The Trip to Pitschepatsch*, 1968) combined real and fantastic elements to demonstrate how a child can learn to master his or her destiny while on a traditional quest. *Stokkerlok und Millipilli* (1969), while also characterized by bizarre and childish features, went a step further in displaying how a girl can use her talents as well as boys and how all the children can unite to fight against authoritarian figures who want to destroy their toys and games, in this case, a locomotive. It was with the production of *Stokkerlok and Millipilli* that Ludwig and the actors from the Reichskabarett, who had been performing largely for adults, decided to take over the children's theater which had been abandoned by Hackenberg and her followers. The beginning was inauspicious since *Stokkerlok and Millipilli* received devastating reviews from the Berlin press. However, six months later this play was awarded the Brothers Grimm prize of Berlin, and in 1970 *Theater heute* awarded it first prize in a contest for children's dramas. This slow and gradual success led the members of the Reichskabarett to devote more time and energy into promoting a new sort of children's play which also corresponded to the anti-authoritarian phase of the student movement. This was the period when the German SDS was reaching its pinnacle and when students were actively using all kinds of methods, violent and pacifistic, to oppose the authoritarian forces in West Germany, in many cases without conceiving long-range programs of how to develop new and durable emancipatory forms of education. The institutions of arbitrary power were to be smashed and were being smashed.

It was in this spirit that *Maximilian Pfeiferling* (1969) was written by Carsten Krüger and Ludwig. This comedy is set in an apartment complex in contemporary Germany. Little Max, as the youngest in the family, is constantly "hassled" and exploited by his older sister, mother and father. Only his uncle supports and encourages him to develop his play instinct, but there is little room for him to play in and around the apartment building, especially since the landlord Herr Brühler (Mr. Yeller) constantly prevents him from playing on his property and even resorts to stealing his toys. Since Max has lost one of his front teeth, he discovers that he has a shrill whistle which he can use as a weapon against his family and Mr. Brühler because the noise hurts their ears. Max soon learns to use his whistle effectively to obtain what he wants, and he finally exposes Mr. Brühler as a thief. The play ends with a demonstration of "children's power," which is portrayed as good and necessary for children if they want to defend their rights. On the other hand, it is somewhat unrealistic since such power is hardly within reach or realization of most children. Here the fact that the family comes to respect and support Maximilian in his struggle against the landlord qualifies the unrealistic aspect of children's power.

Maximilian Pfeiferling was followed by another play written in the anti-authoritarian vein, *Mugnog-Kinder!* (1970) by Rainer Hachfeld, with songs by Ludwig and music by Birger Heymann. Instead of a

shrill whistle, Hachfeld invents a box upon which two children imagi-
natively bestow their own *Grips*, so to speak, their own common sense
and ingenuity. Whenever adults arbitrarily order them to do
something, they respond by asserting, "Mugnog told us it could be
done another way" — generally a way more in keeping with their needs
and desires. The children and Mugnog turn an entire town upside
down and make fools of all the adults until they get their own way. As
in *Maximilian Pfeiferling,* the issue at hand is children's power, i.e.,
children versus adults, who are portrayed as personifications of the
enemy without clarifying the social conditions and processes that
bring about such antagonisms.

The anti-authoritarian content of the plays themselves were not
without an effect on the ensemble itself. The exploration of the
problems confronting children also led to an exploration of the
problems confronting members of the ensemble who sought more
freedom and responsibility as well as new forms of emancipatory
organization within the theater. These struggles within the ensemble
had their parallels in the development of the student movement itself
where there was a discernible trend toward more concrete socialist
programs instead of short-sighted anti-authoritarian action. In
particular, the discovery of Asja Lacis' and Walter Benjamin's
writings on children's theater, the socialist theories of education
developed by Edwin Hoernle, Otto Rühle, Makarenko, Otto Kranitz,
and the psychological studies of Wilhelm Reich, Siegfried Bernfeld,
Vera Schmidt, and members of the Frankfurt School had both a direct
and indirect influence on the members of Grips. This could definitely
be sensed in *Balle, Malle, Hupe und Artur (Bizzy, Dizzy, Daffy and
Arthur,* 1971), written by Dagmar Dorsten, Uli Gressieker, Volker
Ludwig, Stefan Ostertag, Carsten Krüger, and the premiere cast. As
the first play to be written in a collective manner, it revealed a sub-
stantial change in theme, which included working class perspectives
and attitudes toward solidarity. Here four children, who are unable to
find a place to play in the city, discover an abandoned building which
they begin to explore. However, they are arrested by two policemen
and brought to the precinct. Upon interrogation, the children exhibit
strong solidarity and do not allow the police to divide them or pit one
against another. On the contrary, their own actions and questions lead
one of the policemen to side with the children and to see the logic of
their request to convert the abandoned building into a youth center.
There are three important dramaturgical changes in this play which
denote the shift in thematic emphasis. First, one of the four children,

Arthur, is used as a foil for the others, who are more conscious of their oppression and realize the importance of working in a collective manner. Arthur (who represents the audience to a certain extent) must learn to stop being egocentric, to share, and to develop a sense of responsibility for his playmates which in turn brings him great comfort and pleasure. As he learns, so does the audience. Secondly, the adults in this play are differentiated, and one policeman clearly changes his position to support the children. As a figure of authority, the policeman can use his power in a constructive way, and the audience can see that authority is not necessarily negative by nature. Thirdly, Ludwig's songs were no longer embedded in the action of the play but were used to break and comment on the action. As in Brecht's plays, the performers stepped out of their roles and encouraged the audience to sing along, often with printed texts, so that the meaning of the songs would stay with the children.

The dramaturgical changes in *Balle, Malle, Hupe und Artur* were, of course, signs of how the Reichskabarett itself was growing through internal struggles. From this point on, Ludwig and the majority of the actors and technicians decided to devote themselves completely to children's theater and to developing *collective* forms of writing and producing their plays. Since political and personal disputes often slowed production, the decision brought with it immense difficulties. Nevertheless, the cabaret for adults was abandoned, and in November of 1971, the ensemble performed *Trummi Kaputt*, written mainly by Ludwig with the help of the cast, as their last play at their old proscenium theater on Ludwigkirchstrasse. *Trummi Kaputt* marked another advance for the ensemble since it is a more explicit socialist critique of exploitative conditions under capitalism. Bobby Trumm (who functions as Arthur did in the previous play) is the son of a toy manufacturer. He constantly lords his wealth over three other children and frequently charges them money to borrow his toys. When one of them breaks his toy named Trummi, the boy's mother, who happens to work at the toy factory, tries to help him by stealing a replacement. For this she is fired. The children attempt to help her, and since they are disgusted with Bobby and his father, they refuse to play with Bobby and invent their own imaginary game which does not involve manufactured toys. Bobby does not like the feeling of being excluded and tells his father about the wonderful game that has been invented. The father wants to buy the game, but the children refuse to demonstrate how it works until he agrees to rehire the mother. However, the father becomes angry and frustrated when he sees that he cannot manufacture such a game and wants to drag his son home. Bobby rebels because he needs companionship which his father has never provided. The other children and the mother support him at this critical moment. Through their solidarity with his plight, they show him how he can withstand his father's negligent treatment.

The clear socialist tendency of this play is further developed in what is probably the best production of Grips to date, *Mannomann!* (1972) by Volker Ludwig, Reiner Lücker, and the entire ensemble. Significantly, this play heralded the move of the company to the Forum-Theater on the Kurfürstendamm and the baptism of their new name, Grips Theater for Children. The advantage of the new theater was that, as a theater in the round without fixed sets and seats, it allowed for greater contact with the children and more freedom of movement. Some of the actors were concerned that the children might want to participate too much in the production and disrupt the performances, but this "fear" proved to be unfounded. The new move involved other difficulties which were tied more to the contents and interpretation of *Mannomann!*

For the first time an entire play was to be devoted to the women's question, that is, to the problems of the adult world which were to be seen from a children's perspective as directly related to their sphere of activities. The women in the ensemble played an important part in the conception of the play and forced the rewriting of many of the incidents. This also led to long intense political discussions by all members of the group about women's oppression and workers' mentality which caused delays in the production. Though exhausting and nerve-wracking for the entire ensemble, the result was worth it: *Mannomann!* effectively brings the seemingly disparate elements of children's, women's, and workers' oppression into focus and points to the private ownership of property and arbitrary control of production as the main cause for this oppression. Here a single woman learns that the struggles of her children to understand why their step-father mistreats them are her struggles as well. The emphasis in this play is again on solidarity. The children join together with their mother and father to fend off the "representatives" of the capitalist system—a money-grubbing landlord, a frustrated petty gossip, a slick salesman, a bossy foreman. The family changes itself around (the process of *Umfunktionierung*) right before the audience's eyes which gives a new dimension to the concept of role-playing. The Grips ensemble does not merely show that children and adults become more free and talented by playing different roles, but it points out socially and materially why roles can be shared and used to support one another to bring about concrete measures of social freedom.

Since 1973, Grips has endeavored to address itself to actual social problems and to present possible solutions to problems which they consider of a pressing nature. The next play *Doof bleibt doof* (*Once a Dummy, Always a Dummy*, 1973) by Ulrich Gressieker, Volker Ludwig, and Reiner Lücker concerns a young boy in junior high school who is constantly picked on by his young friends because he was flunked and is apparently dumb. Brille, the young boy's nickname, which denotes someone who wears glasses, is more or less the scapegoat for his schoolmates, who take their frustrations out on him. The reason why Brille does so poorly in school is because he is shunned at home by his mother and is obligated to carry out tasks for her. When the other children learn this and also hear that they are in danger of being flunked along with Brille, they begin to support him and hold a mock trial against their teacher, who explains to them that his hands are tied because the large size of the class prevents him from teaching effectively. In other words, the system does not allow him to educate but forces him to be a disciplinarian against his will. The play ends on this note. There is no solution, but the contradictions in the school system are laid bare and questions are posed in this play which school children and their teachers can learn to solve together. Here Grips provides additional help with the publication of the play and material which examines the problem and can be used in schools.

In *Ein Fest bei Papadakis* (*Papadakis Throws a Party*, 1973) by Volker Ludwig, Christian Sorge, and the ensemble, Grips turned to a more solvable problem, the racist attitudes of many Germans toward the "Gastarbeiter," so-called "guest workers," a euphemistic term for immigrant laborers. More than any other Western European country since 1945, West Germany has depended on an enormous influx of immigrant workers to rebuild industry. Greeks, Turks, Arabs, Yugoslavians, Italians, and Spaniards have, due to the wretched conditions in their own countries, come to West Germany to find a means of support for themselves and their families. Given the residue of anti-Semitism in West Germany and the continuation of capitalist work conditions which makes it seem that the foreign workers are threats, great antagonisms have arisen between the German and immigrant workers. In particular the immigrant laborers have been charged exhorbitant rents for bad housing, given lower wages than the German workers, ostracized from the social and cultural life, and generally made to feel inferior to the Germans. *Ein Fest bei Papadakis* tries expressly to explain to children why all this has come about. Not only has the play been successful in its own theater, but it has been effective in schools where a special handbook has been published and distributed by Grips for teachers and children to explore these problems in greater detail. The play itself concerns Papadakis, a Greek worker, and his son Jannis, who encounter Willi Müller, a German worker, and his son and daughter Dieter and Vera on a weekend camping trip. Müller immediately becomes angry at Papadakis, who has unknowingly taken Müller's customary camping site. This leads Müller to utter all the racist clichés about foreign workers he knows and to keep his son and daughter from playing with Jannis. Due to his blind hatred, Müller even has a Turkish girl, who is hired to clean the grounds, fired because she is working illegally. However, here he goes one step too far, for the proprietor of the camping grounds depends on the cheap labor of foreign workers, and he orders Müller off the camping grounds for exposing him. But Papadakis comes to Müller's rescue by pointing out how the owner has overcharged Papadakis as a foreigner for his site, and this, too, is illegal. The families of Papadakis and Müller unite to confront the owner and also to help the Turkish girl, who will return to school with the other children, enabling her to develop her knowledge and skills so that she can fend for herself.

In *Ruhe im Karton!* (*Quiet in the Box!* 1974) written by Stefan Reisner, a new author for Grips, a problem, which was treated in *Mugnog-Kinder!* in an anti-authoritarian manner, is now depicted as having a more collective solution. Two children are continually bossed around by their parents who never listen to their needs but merely want to be left in peace. The two children vent their frustration on their friend Klaus, who always falls for their tricks. When Klaus begins to defend himself, he forces the brother and sister to confront their parents, who in turn learn that they can have more peace and pleasure by responding to their children's *real* needs and desires.

Die Ruckzuckmachine (*The Rickety-rackety Machine*, 1974) by Reiner Lücker and Stefan Reisner is also a more concentrated version of conditions at the work place which were first treated in *Trummi Kaputt* and *Mannomann!* Here, slapstick is used to show how workers who operate a conveyor belt have become alienated from their labor and as robot-like as the machines they serve. Gradually it dawns on the workers that they can turn things around and gain a certain amount of pleasure from their work. In the end, they demonstrate the necessity for workers' control and co-determination at work places.

Neither one of the last two plays mark a great advance over the earlier Grips plays, and it has become evident that the ensemble (while it continues to work collectively in changing and reworking the comedies written first by one or two people) needs more playwrights. In addition, Ludwig, who undoubtedly is the most talented of the dramatists, needs more spare time to concentrate on his writing. Until now he has also been the business manager of the theater, and this has frequently interfered with his writing. For instance, during the summer of 1974, Grips bought and renovated a movie house at Hansa Platz, and Ludwig was in charge of the entire operation. At the same time, he was expected to finish a manuscript for the premiere in the new expansive theater which was eventually held on October 7. Together with Jörg Friedrich, now one of the leading directors of the ensemble, and with the help of the collective, but, as usual, always under the pressure of a deadline, the play was finished. *Nashörner schiessen nicht* (*Rhinoceroces Don't Shoot*) is the first "love story" produced by Grips for children nine years and older. It concerns Wolfgang Hannemann and his father, a worker, who pastes advertisements on walls and billboards. Unlike his father, who is very much down to earth (due to the work he does), Wolfgang is a dreamer, and he becomes romantically attracted to Pia Steinberg, who comes from a wealthy family. Ashamed of his father, Wolfgang seeks the better things in life, and the better things are just those commodities which his father pastes on walls as advertisements. In this regard, Pia also comes to represent the rich, exquisite living style he dreams about. When Wolfgang visits Pia at her home, it turns out that her father, an advertising agent, needs someone just like him to do a tv advertisement. He agrees, thinking that he will become a rich movie star, but it soon becomes apparent that the father intends to underpay and exploit him and another girl from the working class. The father's cheap business tricks are eventually exposed by Wolfgang's father, who comes to fetch his son and sees through the machinations of the advertising agent. By supporting his son and taking a firm stand against exploitation, the father helps bring his son's expectations down to reality, and Wolfgang learns the meaning between the *real* needs of his imagination and the false needs contrived by the advertisement business.

In almost all the Grips plays, including *Nashörner schiessen nicht*, there is a strong tendency to question the traditional roles which boys and girls are expected to play, usually to their detriment. These expected roles are demonstrated through role-playing within the story to be ludicrous, oppressive, and senseless so that the children in the audience can learn to create their own tasks and develop their own talents out of needs which they themselves feel and deduce. The play which has dealt with this problematic most thoroughly has been *Mensch Mädchen!* (*My God, Girl!*). Written by Stefan Reisner for children five years and older, the play was first performed on February 28, 1975, and it has drawn large audiences to the theater at Hansaplatz. Here three girls Ulrike, Gaby, and Sabine decide to build a rocket to the moon on an empty lot. However, when they ask their parents and relatives to lend them tools to build their rocket, they are mocked and refused because little girls are not supposed to build things. Girls are not supposed to get themselves dirty and work with mechanical things. Nevertheless, the girls persist and find tools. As they try to build their rocket, they are constantly interrupted by Bruno, a pesty boy, who steals and destroys their assembled equipment. Finally, they unite and teach him a lesson. After his defeat, he complains that girls have an easier life than boys. The girls disagree, and they all decide to make an experiment. Bruno changes clothes with one of the girls. In his female outfit he is subjected to some absurd treatment by adults and learns how irrationally girls are treated, as does one of the girls learn how boys suffer role manipulation. In the end, Bruno joins with the girls to help them protect their rocket from his own father who wants to take over the empty lot as a parking place for his car. The father is only temporarily defeated, but at the same time, the fighting spirit of collectivity among the girls and Bruno is kept very much alive. Here again Grips stresses a *realistic* appraisal of children's actual situation. Nothing is forced in the play even though the examples of role-playing are contrived. The contriving is an assimilation of real situations; the approach is open-minded; the conclusion is open-ended. Whatever clarity is achieved in the drama emanates from the clear focus on the need to recognize children's needs and rights.

While most Grips plays retain the idealist moment of hope that social relations and hence people themselves can be qualitatively changed, they are at the same time eminently sober and concrete in that they avoid fairy-tale endings. The purpose of the plays is to provoke clear-headed, imaginative thinking on the part of children.

Yet, Grips is not to be thought of exclusively as a children's theater. Its plays have a broad appeal, and more recently, Grips has addressed itself to the problems of teenagers. This is in part due to the continuous maltreatment of teenagers in West Germany, who have suffered enormous oppression during the recent economic recession. The austerity program set up by the West German government has led to greater political and sexual repression at the schools, poor teaching and learning conditions, and the promise of unemployment or undesirable labor for those who graduate at sixteen or seventeen—this means the majority of German teenagers. The result is that adolescents are becoming more and more frustrated by school and work and are at the mercy of a socio-economic system which is geared to groom them *not* to think and use their talents, but to function as hapless tools.

With *Das hälste ja im Kopf nicht aus* (*You Can't Possibly Stand Something Like That*) written by Volker Ludwig and Detlef Michel and performed on September 18, 1975 for the first time, Grips embarked on an ambitious undertaking which again reveals just how committed the ensemble is to principles of an emancipatory theater. The drama focuses mainly on the Kovalevski family: Karl, 36 years old, a truck driver; his wife Elsa, 34, who has a part-time job; Klaus-Dieter, 17, an apprentice at the post office; Thomas, 15, and Martina, 13, who attend a nearby high school. Most of their time together is spent yelling and fighting. No one attempts to understand the other's problems. It is not until there is difficulty at the school because a student rebels while doing meaningless work as a temporary apprentice at a department store that the family is drawn together. The student, Charlie Braun, has only expressed what Thomas, Martina, and their friends feel: school is merely training them for jobs they don't want, and they are being cut off from realizing their own potential and seeking possibilities for their development in society. Spurred on by a young teacher, Helga Schmidt, the students organize strikes and protests to prevent Charlie Braun from being evicted from the school. The teacher herself is threatened by political repression. However, she seeks the support of parents, colleagues, and her union. The Kovalevski family becomes drawn into the struggle and comes to recognize itself as a solid unit by the end of the play. There is no apparent victory, but the students are busy organizing for the next stage of their struggle against the school administration.

Again, a play without a resolution, just as the situation in West

Germany offers no clear solution. Nevertheless, *Das hälste ja im Kopf nicht aus* points the way to alternatives for affirmative action in the interests of different oppressed groups—the students, progressive teachers, and working class families. It also exposes the close connections between businesses and the education system so that the targets for the protest action become more clear. Audiences cannot be left with a sense of helplessness at the end of this play. On the contrary, the dramatic action aids in recovering one's sense of power and effectiveness. Here the staging and rhythm of the drama are important. In the background on an elevated stage there is a rock band of young musicians who play accompaniment to the songs which speak the minds of the teenagers who refuse to put up with a system that, in their minds, just plain stinks. The music stresses through its beat the ideas and dreams which the teenagers often keep down. The tunes carry the realization of their wishes just as the action of the play and the terse dialogue carry forth a program of concrete hope that announces emancipation as the best possible alternative they can choose for their future lives.

It is quite apparent from the contents of the Grips plays that they are emancipatory in a socialist sense. But, are they effective? Or, can they be effective in helping children to become critically conscious of their own talents and the social conditions forging them? It is difficult to generalize in answering this question, for the answer depends on the educational and cultural policies within a particular society. In the specific case of West Berlin, conditions fluctuate a great deal. At the beginning, they were conducive for the development not only of Grips, which is partially subsidized by the city, but for other children's theaters as well which differ in orientation. For instance, since 1969 Helme Ebert and Volkhardt Paris have been experimenting with a theater *for and by* children which incorporate ideas of Edwin Hoernle, Walter Benjamin, and Asja Lacis. This group is called the Kindertheater im Märkischen Viertel, located in a working class district in West Berlin, and it endeavors to help children develop their skills of observation and expression, discuss their personal problems as social problems, do improvised skits about them, and finally to work out possible solutions through performances. This theater has in turn influenced other small groups in West Germany as well as educators who have tried to develop new theories and practices involving role-playing.

Still, it is Grips, which has primarily set the pace for a new emancipatory theater in West Berlin and West Germany. Two groups, Die Rote Grütze and Die Birne, which have recently received attention because of their remarkable plays centering on sexual education and criminal justice, owe a great deal to Grips in regard to their themes and theatrical practice. Other theaters in West Germany like the Theater am Turm (TAT) in Frankfurt are modelling their work on Grips. Almost all the Grips plays have been televised and reproduced by other theaters for children in West Germany and other countries as well. The success of the Grips plays has prompted more playwrights to concentrate on children's theater, and, in some cases, has led to the formation of a children's theater group which exclusively performs Grips plays, as in Hamburg. Most important for the effectiveness of Grips itself in West Berlin is its accent on continuity. Without long, continuous work with young audiences and educators the Grips plays will remain ineffective. The ensemble is highly aware of this, and it is for this reason that it has produced records, books, and teaching manuals to complement the performances. Furthermore, Grips endeavors to cooperate with teachers who carry on their work in the schools themselves. Though it is still too early to tell how great an effect Grips has had, the fact that the company has sought to endow its productions with continuity and to branch out beyond the theater has already made it the most potent and stimulating force in German children's theater.

However, for the most part, Grips remains exceptional, and this is due in large part to the negative attitude of West German society and western capitalist countries which (rightly so) view children's emancipation as a prelude to working class emancipation, or revolution of one kind or another. Even in West Berlin, where I have noted that conditions were conducive for socialist children's theater, Grips *has had to fight for* and *must continue* to fight for every penny of its subsidy and for admission into schools. At present, due to the swing to the Right in West German politics and the McCarthy-like witch hunt of progressive teachers, Grips is being branded as treacherous, communistic, unhealthy, and dangerous. Teachers who bring their children on field trips to performances at the Grips theater are in danger of losing their jobs. The plays have a great deal of difficulty being produced in the south of Germany, the bastion of conservatism. To a certain extent, this notoriety has made audiences more curious about Grips. Yet, more important is that the quality and power of the plays have not decreased, and the ensemble's continued fame and popularity depend more on its rigorous program of emancipatory theater. The Grips plays open the way to new possibilities dramaturgically and socially for experiments within theater which may eventually contribute to pedagogical and social change. It is in this sense that Grips is a model for children's theater in America, and its experiments can be adapted to the specific needs of a given children's theater and community. Here it is important that the basic emancipatory features and tendencies of Grips are not suppressed or played down.

As was mentioned before, Grips is not just a children's theater. It encompasses all of theater, and in this sense, it is truly emancipatory since it relates children's problems of freedom to the problems of freedom and collectivity in the society at large. The public performances of the Grips theater are, in fact, public intrusions in behalf of children's emancipation into the repressive bourgeois public sphere, and here is where it is related to the proletarian struggle for greater social emancipation. Therefore, children's problems are not staged diminutively but comprehensively to draw the disparate, seemingly contradictory social conditions together which affect child and parent alike. This is immediately grasped by all audiences of every age group attending a Grips production, whether consciously or unconsciously.

How does the Grips ensemble bring this about? Almost all of their plays are Brechtian *Lehrstücke* (learning plays), which are performed in a cabaret style that enhances the estrangement effect and allows for pleasure in learning. This means that the actors do *not* try to mimic children or act naturalistically. On the contrary. Social conditions and events are *explained* and *demonstrated* from a children's point of view based on socialist principles which the actors themselves have been trying to elaborate. The plays do not present *final* solutions to problems but show *possible* alternatives to conditions which are oppressive or self-defeating. The plays are not ends in themselves, but means to stimulate audiences how to develop dialectical thinking. In other words, the plays do not preach answers, nor should they be performed this way. They want to teach how enjoyable it can be to master critical thinking which will allow each individual in concrete social situations to pose questions whose solutions bring about greater class solidarity and freedom.

Each scene of a Grips play tends to be a social experiment, a testing of the social conditions to see if perhaps some other form of organization might make more sense and allow for more freedom of movement and development. Characters represent antagonistic principles, and as the characters are unmasked, the processes underlying the principles become more visible, as in the case of the step-father in *Mannomann!* Although he represents male chauvinism, it is not enough to label him simply a male chauvinist but to demonstrate what the social conditions are which contribute to his bias. The actors step out of their roles to show what the conditions are and how they act upon people in given circumstances. The songs of the plays further illustrate the importance of developing a critical method, an approach to a problem, rather than easy solutions. The remarkable music composed by Birger Heymann allows audiences to retain catch-phrases, and it also lends to emphasizing the politics of the lyrics by its unusual beat and juxtapositions. Heymann's rich melodic intonations and abrupt breaks suggest the variations possible for the characters seeking new ways to make their lives more joyful. It is this joy in change that the music conveys through its energetic elements. The style is earthy. There are no illusions created, rather rhythms responding to the reality of the situation undergoing change through play.

It should be stressed that the cabaret style of performing has been the dominant influence on all the actors and the playwrights as well, especially Volker Ludwig. This is important to note since there has been an attempt by certain German academicians and critics to theorize about the dramaturgy of the Grips ensemble and to endow the group with insights and ideas they never knew they had. It is true, as I have already remarked, that the student movement and the rediscovery of theories from the 1920s had an influence on the Grips people. Yet, their origins in the cabaret have ultimately (and perhaps fortunately) marked their exceptional production style. By its very nature the cabaret style is illusion-smashing, frank, quick, jovial, and yet, serious. The actors make no bones about who they really are as actors. Momentarily they want to show how contradictory a social situation is and to provoke an audience to enjoy this realization by using their heads and to think about the serious consequences. The songs elaborate or summarize the thrust of the skit. Good cabaret skits are *Lehrstücke*, and, if we recall that Brecht did his apprenticeship with one of the masters of the cabaret, Karl Valentin, we can see the remarkable connections of his *Lehrstücke* to the cabaret, and the Grips plays to Brecht's *Lehrstücke*.

Grips plays are questions which are disturbing. Naturally they can be played down in a production. This has happened to most of Brecht's plays, both in the East and the West. The Grips ensemble has not allowed this to happen, for their theater work is praxis in the full socialist sense of the word: it involves the acting out and testing of theory in an endeavor to bring about fruitful change. At present, there are two Grips ensembles, one which performs at the home theater, and one which tours schools, churches, and other institutions. In addition, the actors speak with teachers and children about the substance of the plays and have also arranged (as in the case of *Doof bleibt doof, Papadakis, Die Ruckzuckmachine, Mensch Mädchen*, and *Nashörner schiessen nicht*) for small publications to be used in class as educational material. The plays which they perform represent the products of real collective work with which they identify. This collective work has been difficult, and, as the history of the theater reveals, is not entirely "collective" in the purest sense of the word. Yet, the historical struggle of the Grips people to develop collective theater work is exemplary, and their experiments with emancipatory theater have brought children's theater to a new stage which paradoxically may mark the end of children's theater as we have come to know it.

MUGNOG

Original title: *Mugnog-Kinder!* by Rainer Hachfeld. English translation by Jack Zipes and Pamela Bro-Harrison.

Characters:

Actress 1, *Pam*
Actress 2, *Aunt Molly, teacher*
Actor 1, *Tom*
Actor 2, *Uncle Henry, doctor*
Actor 3, *Uniform Man, tv man, policeman, general*
Actor 4, *Crab, Schmuck, mayor, President's assistant*
Guitarist

Note: The play has been written in such a way that all the roles can be played by six actors.

*The stage is in a mess. The two children Tom
and Pam carry a small box onto the stage.*

Tom: Nobody here yet.

Pam: Just take a look at this mess!!

Tom (*towards the rear*): Hey, where is everyone? C'mon out
    wherever you are!

(*Uncle, aunt, Crab, and uniform man enter.*)

Uncle: What's the matter?

Pam: We want to put on a play!

Aunt: Oh, that's neat. I love plays. I'll be the princess!

Tom: Forget it. There's not gonna be a princess or a queen.
    You'll play the aunt.

Aunt: The aunt!!

Pam: Yes, here's your costume. (*She gives her an apron from
    the box.*)

Uncle: Ha-ha, the aunt! And who's gonna play the uncle? You
    think I will?

Tom: Why not, since you're so smart. These glasses will make
    you look even extra smart. Here! (*Gives him the glasses.*)

Uniform man: And me? I want a uniform. I want to be the
    general! Or at least the king!

Pam: If you want to be the big-shot around here, then first
    you have to clean up all this mess.

Uniform man: You want me to clean up. (*Looks around.*) Oh,
    you mean this stuff here. Nothing to it! Watch my dust!
    (*He makes more of a mess instead of cleaning up.*)

Crab: This is all ridiculous! Uncle, aunt, general!! What's all
    this supposed to mean? Those are no kind of roles. I'll tell
    you how to do things, but you've got to let me play the
    knight in shining armor or some kind of a western hero
    like Billy the Kid or Buffalo Bill.

Pam: You'll play Crab.

Crab: What? Crab! You think I'm some kind of a fish or something!

Tom: A crab isn't a fish, it's someone who crabs all the time.

Crab: Damn it all! Who's crabbing around here?

Tom and Pam: Crab!

Crab: I'm not playing your stupid game! (*Exits.*)

Aunt: He'll be back.

Pam: That's what I'm afraid of.

Uncle: Now tell us our names.

Tom: You're Mr. and Mrs. Mackepeter, and we call you Uncle Henry and Aunt Molly.

Aunt: Mackepeter? What a ridiculous name!

Pam: But you look like the Mackepeters.

Uncle: Really? Let me take a look. I need a mirror. (*Exits.*)

Aunt: Me, too. (*Exits.*)

Uniform man: Now will you give me my uniform!

Tom: Have you cleaned up the mess?

Uniform man: Look for yourself.

Tom: That's not exactly the best job in the world.

Uniform man: I'll do better next time. —Maybe. (*Crosses his fingers behind his back.*)

Pam: That's what they all say.

Tom: Just like a general or a king—they always make a lot of noise and pretend, and it always turns out that they're nothing but hot air.

Pam (*takes a cap from a uniform out of the box*): Here you are, general! (*The general makes some silly gestures like soldiers normally do and marches off the stage.*)

Guitarist (*meanders onto the stage*): Hi! How're you doing?

Tom: What do you want here?

Guitarist: I'd like to play, too, if you don't mind.

Pam: But we don't have a role for you.

Tom: Gee, we should be able to find something for him to play.

Guitarist: The guitar!

Pam: The guitar. You mean you really can play the guitar?

Tom: Of course! Anyone can play the guitar. (*The guitarist sits down on the stage and begins to play softly.*)

Pam: What now?

Tom: Now what?...(*To the guitarist*): Play something nice to help us clean up the mess here. (*Tom and Pam make the stage into a living room in time to the music.*)

Tom: By the way, what's your name?

Pam: Margie.

Tom: I know that. I mean, what name are you going to use in the play?

Pam: Ummm—I don't know.

Tom: Then I'll just call you Pam the wham!

Pam: Oh yeah, well, I'll just call you Tom the Cat!

Tom: Oh yeah, well then, I'll just call you Pam for short.

Pam: And I'll just call you Tom.

Crab (*comes rushing onto the stage*): Everyone has a role except me. That's not fair. I want something, too! The others got glasses and a cap. At least give me an apron, or...or...a gun!

Tom: Look at him crabbing away!

Pam: So he came back after all.

Crab: C'mon now, give me one of your cruddy things! Where'd you put my costume?

Tom: Look in the box.

Crab (*sticks his hand into the box and pulls out a beard which he drops in a hurry. Horrified*): Eiiiiii! What is it? A bug?! Disgusting!!

Pam: That's a beard.

Tom: It's what we call a crab beard.

Crab (*takes the beard and holds it up under his nose*): A-choo! A-choo!

Pam: Gesundheit!

Crab: Well, how do I look?

Tom: Just like all crabs look. But now you look more like Mr. Schmuck.

Pam: Well, after all, that's one of his roles, too.

Crab: Schmuck! What kind of stupid names are you giving me? Crab! Schmuck!—What about you two? What roles are you playing?

Pam: We're the children. Can't you see?

Schmuck: Now I get it... You always take the best roles for yourselves.

Tom: But Mr. Schmuck isn't a bad role.

Schmuck: Are you kidding? With a name like that! And what am I supposed to do?

Pam: You can't stand us.

Schmuck: That's not true. I was only mad because...

Tom: You don't get the point. It's Mr. Schmuck who can't stand us.

Schmuck: Oh, now I understand. But how come?

Pam: Well, you see, we're on vacation from school, and we're visiting our aunt and uncle the Mackepeters in this small city where they live. In fact, they live right upstairs from you, and we're always making noise.

Schmuck: And that always makes me mad.

Tom: Right!

Schmuck: Well, then let's get on with the show.... We don't need this stupid box anymore! (*Wants to move it off the stage.*)

Pam: Stop!! (*Schmuck jumps in fright.*)

Schmuck: What now?

Pam: This box has the most important role in the play.

Schmuck: The box?

Pam: That's not a box, dummy. That's Mugnog!

Schmuck: Mugnog?

Pam: Mugnog's our toy. As children we have to play with something, don't we?

Tom: That's right. A box makes for a really nice toy. You can do all sorts of different things with it. It's the best toy in the world.

Pam: Well, I wouldn't go that far. Mugnog, well that's...well, you know, Mugnog's a Mugnog. Isn't that right, Mr. Schmuck?

Schmuck (*wants to move the box*): You two are whacky!

Tom and *Pam*: Watch out! (*Schmuck jumps back.*)

Pam: It bites.

Schmuck: Who?

Tom: Mugnog. (*Picks Mugnog up and carries it off followed by Pam).*

Schmuck: Mugnog! What nonsense! Mugnog!

Woman 1: What's that?

Schmuck: Mugnog! Mugnog!

Woman 1 (feels his temple): Are you sick?

Schmuck: Mugnog!

Man 2: What's he talking about?

Woman 1: He keeps saying Mudbug.

Schmuck: Wrong! It's Mugnog.

Woman 1 and *Man 2*: What??

Schmuck: The children—the box— I mean—Mugnog—oh, forget it! This is all ridiculous. they've already made me into a blooming fool. *(Exits).*

Woman 1, Aunt: The children!!

Man 2, Uncle: Did he mean our niece and nephew?

Aunt: Where are they hiding themselves anyway?

Uncle: Tom!

Aunt: Pam!

Tom and Pam: Hi, Aunt Molly, hi, Uncle Henry!

Uncle: There you are!

Aunt: All right now I want you to go and wash up and get ready for bed. Hurry now, and don't splash water on the floor.

Uncle: And no noise. Otherwise Mr. Schmuck will come up here and complain again.

Tom: Mugnog says that Mr. Schmuck's a dumb old fool.

Uncle: Hey, now, where are your manners? Good boys don't say things like that. I don't ever want to hear that from you again.

Pam: But we never said it. It was Mugnog. *(Exits with Tom.)*

Aunt: There's that word again!

Uncle: Mugnog—strange.

(Noise is heard from the bathroom. Tom and Pam sing loudly and giggle.)

Aunt: Just listen to them!

Uncle (runs to the door): Hey, you two, keep quiet in there.

(*The doorbell rings.*)

Aunt: Oh-oh, it's too late already.

Uncle: Leave it to me. (*Goes to the door. Mr. Schmuck enters.*)

Schmuck: Can't you keep those children quiet?

Uncle: I know, Mr. Schmuck. I'm really sorry, but we're suffering just as much as you are.

Schmuck: You want my advice: wallop the daylights out of them! (*As he is talking, Tom and Pam enter.*) And if you can't do the job, just leave it to me. I'll take care of the dear little brats.

Uncle (*to Tom and Pam*): You heard what Mr. Schmuck said. So now you'd better behave yourselves.

Aunt: You have to be a little more quiet.

Uncle: No more singing!

Schmuck: No more playing!

Uncle: Otherwise —

Aunt: Otherwise —

Schmuck: Otherwise, there'll be nothing left to do except wallop the daylights out of you two. (*Exits.*)

Pam: What a crab!

Tom: Only a crab could play Mr. Schmuck. That's just the role for him.

Pam: We've got to tell Mugnog that.

Uncle: While we're on the subject, you wouldn't mind showing your Uncle Henry this cute little Mugnog of yours, would you?

Aunt: What a good idea! I'd love to get to know him. Where is he?

Tom: I don't know. Maybe he's gone for a walk?

Pam: Or taken a trip?

Uncle: Tell me, who is Mugnog?

Tom: Mugnog's a Mugnog.

Mugnog Song

Aunt & Uncle: Mugnog? Mugnog? What's it sposed to be?
Mugnog? Mugnog? Is it safe to see?
Things were quiet here, and then —

Mugnog just comes crashing in.
Far and near, all we hear
'til it's coming out our ears.

Pam & Tom: Mugnog! Mugnog!
Pam: Just what Mugnog is and does
Is none of grown-ups' business.
When someone kicks,
Tom: he bites them.
When someone crabs,
Pam: he fights them.
You go to sleep,
Tom: he wakes up.
You start to yell,
Pam: He breaks up.
Pam and Tom: He laughs the whole day through.
But obeying, obeying, obeying,
that he'll never do.

Aunt & Uncle: What is a Mugnog?
It's going to drive us nuts.

Pam & Tom: A Mugnog's just a Mugnog,
and we're just us.
A Mugnog's just a Mugnog,
and we're just us.

Aunt: Aha. Now I get it.
Pam: Really?
Uncle: At any rate this Mugnog is a fresh little thing.
Tom: No, he's got a lot of sense.
Aunt: That's interesting. You've got to show him to us when
he returns, but now it's time for bed!
Pam: Mugnog says that if you're not tired, then you don't have
to go to bed.
Uncle: Mugnog doesn't give the orders around here. I'm the
one you listen to.
Tom: But we're on vacation, and I thought we could just enjoy

ourselves here and not be bossed around. Mugnog says...

Uncle: Now that's enough!

Aunt: Henry, not so loud!...What did Mugnog say, dear?

Tom: Mugnog says that if you're on vacation and visiting people, you can go to bed whenever you want, not when you have to!

Pam: Who wants to go to bed when they're not even tired. That's just plain dumb...

Uncle: Pam!

Pam: That's what Mugnog said.

Aunt: I'll tell you what: we'll talk it over with him.

Tom: With who?

Aunt: With Mugnog.

(*Pam and Tom laugh.*)

Uncle: What are you laughing about? Enough of this silly stuff. Off you go to bed!

Pam: Okay, if that's the way you want it, but when Mugnog learns about this...

Uncle (*yells*): Now cut it out! I don't want to hear one more word about Mugnog. Now out of here! On the double! (*Children exit.*)

Aunt: Not so loud, Henry. Mr. Schmuck will hear you down below.

(*The doorbell rings.*)

Aunt: There he is again. (*She runs to the door.*)

Schmuck: Who's making all that noise? I told you, if they make trouble, wallop the daylights out of them!

Uncle (*extends his rear end*): All right, this time it was me.

Schmuck: You??

Aunt: Please, Mr. Schmuck, it was just too much for my husband to take. Always this Mugnog.

Schmuck: Aha, Mugnog. No wonder there was so much noise. Where is he?

Uncle: Supposedly he's gone on a trip.

Schmuck: What a laugh! (*Laughs.*)

Aunt: Don't tell me that you know Mugnog?

Schmuck: Of course I know him. And how!

Uncle: What? You know him. What kind of a guy is he?

Schmuck: Guy? It's no guy. It's a box.

Aunt: A box??

Schmuck: Or a wooden chest. A lousy box. Nothing more, nothing less. But let me tell you something: if I were you, I wouldn't allow the children to play with it. (*Exits.*)

Uncle: Do you really think it's a box?

Aunt: A box? Maybe....Maybe it's really a portable tv?

Uncle: Of course. That's just like a box. Why didn't we think of that in the first place? A tv set. They're always showing those horrible programs for children. Now they're even telling them that they don't have to go to bed when they should.

Aunt: Disgraceful! The next thing you know, they'll want us to pay for these programs. Henry, call up the tv station and give them a piece of your mind!

Uncle: Wait a second. What if it's really not a tv set? Afterall, Mr. Schmuck said it was a box.

Aunt: Don't be such a coward! It's got to be a tv set. C'mon now. Call them up. Right now!

Uncle: If you think it'll do any good. (*Goes to the telephone, but then hesitates.*) But what if it's really not a...

Aunt (*threatening*): It looks like I'm going to have to do the calling.

Uncle: No, definitely not. I'm the man around here. I'll take care of it. (*Dials.*) Hello. Yes? This is Henry Mackepeter. May I speak to Mugnog please? —Huh—I mean—the tv? Yes? Tell me now, what kind of programs are you showing children? You should be ashamed of yourselves telling children not to go to bed when they should! —What?—You didn't say that?—But what about Mugnog? —No, no, the children told us! No, Mugnog, not Mackmack. I'll spell it for you: M-U-G-N-O-G! That's right, a tv program. No, I don't know what program—yes?—You yourself? Yes—13 Fulton Avenue, apartment 2, Mackepeter. Thank you. (*Hangs up.*) They're sending someone over here.

Aunt: To us? They're coming over to our place?

Uncle: I couldn't do anything about it. He'll be right over.

Aunt: But we don't even have a tv set.

Uncle: Oh, my God! I didn't even think about that. What are we going to say?

Aunt: We'll tell him exactly what the children told us. (*The doorbell rings.*)

Uncle: You think that's him already?

Aunt: Who else could it be? (*The doorbell continues to ring.*) Well, go answer it.

Uncle: No, I'd rather not. (*The doorbell rings again.*) Maybe it's the phone?

Aunt: Don't be so foolish! You know very well that it's the doorbell. Well, I'll answer it myself.

Uncle: Molly!

Aunt: Yeees?

Uncle: What should we tell him?

Aunt: I'll take care of everything. (*She goes to the door.*)

TV Man (*wears a uniform and cap, carries a tv set on his back with wires and antennas, etc.*): Good evening...

Aunt: Are you the...

TV Man: ...the tv man! Someone called me. Do you mind if I put my things down here? (*Puts the set on the floor and his cap on an antenna, takes a long wire.*) So, now let's see what the problem is. Where's your set?

Uncle: Uh—uh—it's on a trip.

TV Man: What?

Aunt: Don't pay any attention to him. Frankly, the reason why we called is because of our niece and nephew. They're spending their vacation with us.

Uncle: And Mugnog, too!

TV Man: What was that?

Aunt: Nothing, nothing. You see, it all happened like this: the children saw this tv program.

TV Man: Aha! Where's the set? (*Looks for it.*)

Uncle: Maybe it only went out for a walk.

Aunt: Keep quiet!

(*The TV Man disappears into the children's room. Suddenly there's a big commotion. The TV Man comes running onto the stage. A pillow is thrown after him. Tom appears in his pajamas.*)

Tom: What's going on here? Who's this guy?

Pam (*also dressed in pajamas, carries a pillow under her arm*): First you make us go to bed when we don't want to, and when we finally fall asleep, some guy shows up and begins fussing around with this wire in my face.

TV Man: I wanted to—I didn't know—

Pam (*takes her pillow and hits the TV Man with it*): Nobody disturbs my sleep and gets away with it!

Tom (*lifts his pillow and begins swinging it at the TV Man*): That's right! We'll teach you to wake us in the middle of the night!

Uncle: Now, stop that, children! Behave yourselves!

Aunt: This is the TV Man!

Tom and Pam (*stop hitting him*): TV Man???

TV Man (*proudly and foolishly, trying to make himself important*): Now, kiddies, kiddies, pay close attention. I've brought you some super selections.

Tom: Da-da-da-da-da-da-da-da-.

Pam (*sings a silly ditty in a false key with a squeaky voice*): "Good morning to you, good morning to you, we're all in our places with sun-shiny faces."

TV Man: Excellent. Ex-cel-lent! Now, kiddies, take a look at this. (*To Aunt and Uncle*): These are our tv shows. (*Takes some pictures from the tv set and shows them to Tom and Pam*): Flowers and horses—funny-looking dolphins and funny-looking lions. Aren't they funny-looking?—cowboys and Indians. Exciting, isn't it?... (*Tom and Pam yawn. Then they start playing with the cord of the tv set.*) You can see for yourself: there is no such thing as a Bugrug on our station's programs.

Aunt: Mugnog!

TV Man: Mugnog—call it what you like. We don't have it.

Pam: That's for sure! Can you imagine our Mugnog on tv?

Tom: Not on your life. He'd never go along with it.

Aunt: But I thought—Mr. Schmuck said it was a box.

Uncle: So naturally, we thought that it was a tv box, I mean, tv set—that you saw a program on tv with Mugnog.

(*Tom and Pam laugh.*)

TV Man: What's all this about? You mean that you don't own
   a tv set?

Aunt and *Uncle*: No.

TV Man (*who becomes bitter and angry*): You mean to tell
   me you called me up for no reason at all! You want me to
   waste my valuable time here when you don't even own a
   tv! The nerve!

Pam: Yes, they've got some nerve!

Tom: They certainly do!

TV Man: TV is the most beautiful thing in the entire world!!
   And you don't have a tv set!

Tom: What did you say? TV may be nice, every now and then.

Pam: Yeah—when you play some good music!

Tom: Or when there's a good adventure story!

Pam: But that's normally when we're sent to bed.

Tom: Yeah, and when your shows come on for children,
   they're pretty stupid. (*Both begin horsing around*): La la
   la la, kiddies, now listen to this, la la la la, kiddies, now
   take a good look.

TV Song

TV Man: When I'm home the tv's always going,
   from early morn right on through the night.
   In every room a tv screen is glowing,
   the toilet and the kitchen sets are bright.

   We watch it while we're eating and we're drinking,
   the soup gets splashed, the rug is like a lake.
   We dribble food until our clothes start stinking,
   and dump salt in our coffee by mistake.

   We clip our fingertips without half caring.
   We never talk, we always sit there staring.
   Our necks are stiff, our eyes turn red.
   And that's our life until we go to bed.

(*He jumps up.*) Oh my God! My stiff neck, my poor eyes!

—I've got to get going. The show's about to start!

Aunt: Which show!

TV Man: How should I know? Anyway, it doesn't matter! The main thing is tv! TV!! I just love tv! (*He packs his things together. In the meantime Pam and Tom have tied knots in the cord so that it can't be undone. The TV Man can't leave.*). Damn it! What's going on here? What have you two done to my cord? Can't you control these monsters? They've ruined everything. I'm going to be late for tv. (*Finally he can untie himself.*) Now let me tell you something: I don't want you to call me ever again until you get yourselves a tv set! Understand? (*The children throw their pillows at him as their way of saying good bye.*) As for these kids, there's something wrong with them. Any sane person can see that. You'd better get them to a doctor, and you'd better do it fast! (*Exits.*)

Uncle: You really think we should get them to a doctor?

Aunt: The children? I don't know. As far as I can see, they're healthy and normal.

Uncle: But this thing with Mugnog....

Pam: Mugnog says...

Pam and Tom: ...that he doesn't need a doctor!

Aunt: Oh, you're still here. Now off to bed, the both of you! (*The children exit.*)

Uncle: Well, I've had it with Mugnog! I've had it up to here! I want you to go get the doctor tomorrow and bring him here.

Aunt: Why me?

Uncle (*falls out of his role*): Don't be so dumb. If I have to play the doctor, then you've got to get him. Or maybe you want Crab or the TV Man to play the doctor?

Aunt: No, not really. I want you to.

Uncle: Well then. —Let's go to sleep. —Mugnog! (*He sings as he leaves*):

> Things were quiet here and then,
> Mugnog just comes crashing in,
> Far and near,
> All we hear...

(*Both exit.*)

The guitarist (*continues to sing*):
>   Just what Mugnog is and does
>   is none of grown-ups' business.
>   A Mugnog's just a Mugnog,
>   and we're just us!
>   A Mugnog's just a Mugnog,
>   and we're just us!

II
Morning

There are two beds against the back wall. The children are lying in the beds. Pam is awake. Tom is still dozing. In between the beds is Mugnog as a night table with a cover on top of it and a lamp on top of the cover.

Pam: Tom! Get up! It's morning. We've got to get up!

Tom: What do you mean "got to, got to?" I hate getting up. Anyway Mugnog's still sleeping.

Pam (*lifts the cover of the night table*): How you doing, Mugnog? Still sleeping? Mugnog's up, too. Good morning, Mugnog!

Tom: You woke him up. That's not nice. We're on vacation, so why don't you let us sleep?

Pam (*hits him over the head with her pillow*): What do you want to do today? Fool around with old Crab?

Tom: We've got to watch out. Crab—I mean, Mr. Schmuck wants to take Mugnog away from us, and so do Aunt Molly and Uncle Henry. They think we're crazy or something.

Pam: Maybe all the children here think so, too.

Tom (*becomes excited, talks to the audience*): Is that true? You think we're crazy??

Pam: I think you should tell them all about Mugnog.

Tom (*has become sleepy again*): You do it. I'm too tired.

Pam (*to the audience*): Okay, I'll do it, but you've got to promise not to tell Mr. Schmuck or Aunt Molly and Uncle Henry. Promise? (*Takes the lamp and cover from Mugnog and holds the box in both hands.*) Well then, Mugnog is merely a box. A plain ordinary box. There's nothing special about it at all.

Tom: Yes, there is. There is something special.

Pam: Yes, but we dreamed that up ourselves. We simply pretend as if Mugnog, I mean, the box, as if it were...well, ...(*to Tom*): You explain it!

Tom: It's simple: I'm sure you've all had teddy bears, or dolls, or stuffed dogs or something like that. And you probably thought of them as being alive. You talk with them and listen to them as if they were real.

Pam: And that's what we do with Mugnog, too.

Tom: I mean, this isn't a doll or teddy bear. But it can also be a lot of fun. Sometimes it's even more fun with a plain old box.

Pam: Grown-ups don't understand. They don't understand at all. And since they don't understand Mugnog...

Tom: ...they freak out.

Pam: And they want to take him, I mean, Mugnog, away from us.

Tom: But they won't succeed.

Pam: We hope. (*Pets Mugnog.*) He's such a nice Mugnog.

Tom: How come we named him Mugnog?

Pam: We made it up. Remember? We could've named him Hot Dog or Moon Dog or Chug-a-log. Mugnog's just a name...

Tom: A real neat name. I like it. Mugnog...

(*Aunt comes into the room. Pam quickly puts Mugnog back in its place. She throws the cover on it but doesn't replace the lamp.*

Aunt: Now what are you two rascals up to? Did you have a good sleep? (*Turns to the door.*) Come right in, doctor. They're up and at it.

Pam: Doctor?

Doctor (*comes into the room*): Have no fear, the doctor's here. Now, now, let's see what the trouble is here.

Tom: Will you take a look at this guy!

Pam: What's he doing here?

Doctor: Your aunt told me that you weren't feeling well.

Aunt: That's not exactly true. I said, it seems as though they might be sick—I mean, only a bit—a tiny bit—(*Exits.*)

Doctor (*sits down on Mugnog*): Well, we'll soon see.

Tom (*softly to Pam*): He's sitting on Mugnog!

Pam (*loudly*): What? You're sitting on Mugnog!

Doctor (*jumps up and holds his behind*): Uaah! What is it?

Tom: Mugnog.

Doctor: Well, well. Hmmm. Is that—is that Mugnog? I mean, is he in that box?

Pam: I give up.

Tom: What do you mean? I don't see any box. I only see Mugnog.

Doctor: Hmmm. (*Examines the box.*)

Tom: Watch out!

Doctor (*jumps backwards*): What's the matter?

Tom: Mugnog doesn't let just any old person touch him.

Pam: Sometimes he bites.

Doctor (*looks back and forth at the children. Suddenly*): Woof! Woof! (*The children become frightened.*) Sometimes I bite too! (*To Pam*): Open your mouth and say: "Ahhh!"

Pam (*opens her mouth*): Ahhh! (*The doctor sticks an apple in her mouth.*)

Doctor (*to Tom*): And you, too. Say "Ahhh!"

Tom (*opens his mouth*): Ahhh! (*The doctor sticks an apple in his mouth, too.*)

Doctor: An apple a day keeps the doctor away, keeps you nice and healthy, just like you are. There's nothing wrong with either one of you. Enjoy your vacation. So long. (*Knocks on top of Mugnog.*) Good bye, Mugnog. (*Exits.*)

Pam (*with the apple in her mouth*): Hmmph, hmmph, hmmph!

Tom (*takes the apple out of his mouth*): What did you say?

Pam (*takes the apple out of her mouth*): You know what? That doctor wasn't so dumb after all, was he?

Tom: But maybe he'll tell on us. Maybe he'll tell them all about Mugnog.

Pam: Not him. He's not the kind. —Now we've really got to get going.

(*Both exit.*)

Aunt: He said they were completely healthy. Completely normal. Just a little bit fresh.

Uncle: What did I tell you! Fresh! That's exactly what I said.

Aunt: Being fresh is no sickness.

Uncle: Sometimes I wish they *were* sick so that they'd be quiet.

Aunt: What a thing to say! You should be ashamed of yourself!

Uncle: But Mr. Schmuck, Mr. Schmuck also said that it'd be better if they just stayed in bed the whole day and didn't make a peep.

Aunt (*horrified*): Mr. Schmuck! —He's always saying horrible things. (*She places the lamp on top of the cover concealing Mugnog.*) Say, Henry, this isn't our night table, is it?

Uncle: What's not our night table?

Aunt: This box here.

Both: Box!!!

Uncle: It's Mugnog. (*Both take a step backward.*)

Aunt: So that's him.

Uncle: Quick. We'll take him away and chop him into little pieces. Let's go. When I count to three, you grab him.

Aunt: Why me?

Uncle (*wants to grab hold of Mugnog but doesn't dare. Finally he examines it carefully*): Actually it's just a plain ordinary box. Made out of wood. What do you think's inside?

Pam and Tom are now completely dressed and sneak into the audience without being heard. They watch their aunt and uncle and signal each other to keep quiet until the right moment.

Aunt: Open it up.

Uncle: You think I should?

Aunt: Are you afraid?

Uncle: Don't be foolish. It's only a box. (*Wants to touch it again, but doesn't dare.*) Maybe there's an animal inside?

Aunt: A cockroach.

Uncle (*shuddering*): Or a poisonous snake. Uaah!

Aunt: Ridiculous! Where could the children have found a poisonous snake.

Uncle: You're right! I'll take a peek inside. (*Touches the top.*)

(*Pam and Tom make strange noises and finally scream.*)

Uncle (*jumps back in fright*): Uaah!

(*Aunt and Uncle run out of the room.*)

Pam: Well, we were lucky again.

Tom: We've got to get Mugnog out of here. Otherwise, they'll steal him for sure!

Pam: Where in the world are we going to hide him? (*Picks up Mugnog. The doorbell rings.*)

Tom: Quick, let's get out of here. We'll take him into the garden.

(*Both exit. Schmuck, Aunt, and Uncle enter.*)

Schmuck: I'm telling you for the last time. Either you give these kids a good licking, or I'm gonna call the police!

Aunt: I can't hit a child.

Schmuck (*to the Uncle*): And you??

Uncle: I don't know. They're both pretty strong and tough. Maybe they'd hit me back.

Schmuck: I can see that you two don't know nothing about raising kids. Where are they anyway?

Aunt (*looks around*): They've gone out—

Uncle: That's good. I'll go get that box and chop it to smithereens. You want to help me?

Schmuck: Do I?! I'll get my saw. First show me where they put the box.

Uncle: Hey, it's not here!

(*Pam and Tom have snuck inside again and begin to laugh.*)

Schmuck (*to the Aunt*): What's there to laugh about? Let me tell you something: you'll never bring these kids under control, especially with this husband of yours, this milkweed over here...

Uncle: Now, wait a moment...
Schmuck: The kids are making a monkey out of you, and you
    won't even give them a good walloping!
Aunt: But!
Schmuck: No "buts, buts," it's their rear ends I'm after!

They're Much Too Loud

Schmuck: They're much too loud!
Pam: They're much too loud!
Tom and Pam: They're much too loud!
(*The grown-ups turn around in surprise.*)
Pam, Tom, and Schmuck: This kind of noise
                          I simply cannot bear.
Schmuck: They're much too fresh!
Tom: They're much too fresh!
Tom and Pam: They're much too fresh!
Pam, Tom, and Schmuck: I'll show them who is boss,
                         Then they won't dare.
Pam: We could all have
    a friendly talk now.
Schmuck: I could just give your skulls a
    knock now!
Tom: Just look at him and you
    can see,
Pam: how silly grown-ups
    get to be.
Tom and Pam: How very silly
    they often get to be.
Schmuck: They're much too loud,
    They're much too loud,
    They're much too loud!

(*Aunt and Uncle stand between them all in embarrassment.*)
Pam: Give their rear ends a good walloping! How dumb can
    you be! I don't even do that to my dolls!
Tom: You really think that children understand grown-ups
    better when their rear ends are beaten?
Schmuck: Poo! I wasn't talking to you, and I don't want to talk

to you two!

Aunt: But maybe you should do that, Mr. Schmuck—every now and then.

Schmuck: It's terrible. The whole thing's terrible.

Pam: What is?

Schmuck: There's only one thing left to do! I'm gonna call the police! Now you'll see some action. I'll have you thrown in jail for disturbing the peace! (*Exits.*)

Tom: That's almost dumber than giving children a good beating.

Uncle: No! For once, I think he's doing the right thing!

Aunt: For heaven's sake. What's gotten into you? Do you want trouble with the police? Now that's really overdoing it a bit.

Uncle: Well, if you ask me, if anyone's overdoing it a bit, then it's Tom and Pam and this—this Mugfog—I mean, Mugdog—

Tom and Pam: Mugnog.

Uncle: Damn it all! Mughog—Mugrug—, Mugnog. I—I don't understand this world anymore! Mugnog... (*Exits with aunt.*)

(*Tom and Pam sing while the sets are changed.*)

> When someone kicks, he bites them.
> When someone crabs, he fights them.
> You go to sleep, he wakes up.
> You start to yell, he breaks up.
> He laughs the whole day through.
> But obeying, obeying, obeying,
> that he'll never do.
>
> A Mugnog's just a Mugnog,
> and we're just us.
> A Mugnog's just a Mugnog,
> and we're just us.

III
The Garden

There is a bench in the middle of the garden. Mugnog is placed on it so that he is clearly visible. To the right of the bench are trees or bushes. Tom and Pam enter carrying Mugnog, and they place him on the bench.

Pam: It's really great to have a garden with flowers and trees. I wish we had one like this at home. But I guess you can't have one in the city.

Tom: That's not true. People have gardens in the city, too. But most of the time they don't let children in because they think children'll ruin the place. They put up fences to keep us out and just lie around in them and sun themselves. Like this! (*He shows her.*)

Garden Song

Pam: I wish I had a garden.
     Lots of people plant them.
     Then they make some signs that say:
     "Children can't come in and play."
     It's not fair.
     It's not fair.
     It's not fair!

     In the lovely gardens
     playing is forbidden.
     Empty gardens, sad and still,
     make no sense and never will—
     Oh how dumb.
     Oh how dumb.
     Oh how dumb!

     One fine day we'll come along and
     tear the fences down and

> throw them all away—
> All the kids will come and play.
> One fine day, one fine day,
> One fine day!

What are gardens made for it they're not made for children!

Pam (*plays a child who wants to play in a garden. She goes over to Tom and curtsies*): May I play in your garden?

Tom (*plays the owner of a house and a garden*): What d'you want? Play in my garden? Have you lost your mind? Just imagine if I let anyone who came by play in my garden!

Pam: Oh, that'd be great!

Tom: What do you mean?

Pam: I'm imagining what would happen if all the people who owned gardens would let all the children who don't have one into their gardens.

Tom: That'd be crazy! All the yelling! All the noise! And they'd trample the flowers and ruin the lawn!! It'd be just plain crazy to let you kids play whereever you wanted to.

Pam: It'd really be great!!

Tom (*as Tom again*): I know, Pam. You're right. That's just the way grown-ups are—anyway that's the way a lot of them are. We should just be glad that we've got this garden to play in during our vacation and that we don't have to play on the streets where someone's always calling the cops to chase us away.

Policeman: Hey, you two over there! Are you Pam and Tom?

Pam: Speak of the devil!

Tom: You think he wants to arrest Mugnog?

Pam: Just let him try!

Policeman: Hey, I asked you something! Up against the wall! (*He frisks them.*) All right, put your hands down!

Tom: Yes, sir. I mean, yes captain.

Policeman (*is flattered*): Well, that's nice of you, but I'm really not a captain—that is, not yet. My name's patrolman Clubb.

Pam: Hi, Mr. Clubb. I'm Pam, and that's Tom.

Policeman (*who quickly becomes official again*): Well now,

Pam and Tom. You're the ones who're always making a racket around here. We can't let that go on. If I hear *one more time* that you're making noise, you'll pay for it.

Tom: What if you hear *three more times?*

Pam: What if you hear *a thousand?*

Policeman: Then, then—someone should give you two a good beating!

Tom: That's what Mr. Schmuck always says.

Policeman: Well, he's right!

Pam: But Mugnog says that Mr. Schmuck is a dumb old fool.

Policeman: Hey now, watch what you're saying! If I tell your uncle that you...

Tom: You know what Mugnog says, Mugnog says that policemen who squeal will never become police chiefs. That's what Mugnog says.

Policeman: What! Me a squealer? I'm gonna run this Mugnog in!

Pam: Did you hear that, Mr. Mugnog? (*Goes to Mugnog and starts talking with it.*) How do you like that, Mr. Mugnog? (*To the policeman*): Mr. Mugnog requests that you call him simply Mugnog.

Policeman (*scratches his head*): I think I'm going off my nut. —What are you two up to? What's that thing over there?

Schmuck (*enters*): Ahhh, there you are! And Mugnog's here, too!

Policeman (*to Schmuck*): What did you say?

Schmuck: There, the box over there. Do you see it? That's Mugnog. That's the thing that started it all. Those two are the ones who make all the noise, but he's the one who starts it all. Now arrest him!

Policeman: Who?

Schmuck: Mug—the box—uhh—the carton—oh, damn it all, Mugnog!

Policeman: I can't arrest him. At most I can confiscate him.

Tom: But that's our Mugnog!

Pam: You'd better leave him here. He bites!

Schmuck: Don't believe a word they say. Confiscate the box. Go on. Otherwise I'll make a complaint to the mayor about you.

Policeman: Okay, cool it. I'll confiscate the box...

Tom: Mugnog.

Policeman: All right, all right, Mugnog! I'll confiscate Mugnog temporarily and bring him to the mayor. But only until everything is cleared up. (*Picks up Mugnog.*)

Just as he picks up Mugnog, the children begin to scream. The policeman does not allow himself to be intimidated. Schmuck holds his hands over his ears.

Policeman (*grins at the children*): Not all cops are as dumb as they look. (*Exits.*)

Tom: Yeah, well, you got to be pretty dumb to arrest Mugnog.

Pam: He's the one to blame!

Schmuck: Me? How come? It was the policeman who...

Tom: But if you hadn't been here...

Pam: You measly toad—you turkey mouth!

Schmuck: What?

Pam: That's what Mugnog would say.

Schmuck: But he's no longer around. Serves you right! Ha-ha-ha! (*Exits.*)

Tom: What do we do now?

Pam: We've got to free Mugnog!

Tom: Right on! (*To the audience*): You think we should do it?

Pam: But how?

Tom: Well, whatever we do, we've got to go to the mayor's office!

Aunt and Uncle enter carrying a table, bowls, plates, and stools in order to eat in the garden.

Aunt: Tomm! Pamm! We've decided to eat outside because it's such a beautiful day. Come, sit down at the table. (*They all take their seats. Aunt serves everyone.*)

Tom (*impatiently*): Actually, I'm not all that hungry.

Pam: Me, neither. Do you mind if we take a walk?

Uncle: What's going on here? It's noon. Time to eat. You

know that.

Aunt: And it's especially important for children to eat a lot so that...

All: They can grow up big and strong.

Aunt: Exactly! So, eat and enjoy your meal!

Tom: That's enough for me.

Uncle: Now cut this out and eat what's on the table.

Tom (*sticks his fork lightly into his uncle's hand and pretends to cut it with his knife*): All right, I'll eat whatever's on the table.

Uncle (*draws his hand back*): Owww! Have you gone crazy or something??

Tom: Your hand was on the table.

Pam (*attempts to eat her plate*): I'm eating whatever's on the table.

Aunt: That's my best dishware! Stop it! That's no way to behave!

Pam: You mean I shouldn't eat whatever's on the table?

Aunt: No, not everything.

Tom: I'm full already!

Pam: Me, too. Can we go now? (*They stand up.*)

Uncle: Finish your meal.

Aunt: You've got to eat something.

Tom: Mugnog says that children should eat only when they're hungry and not when they're forced to.

Uncle: Oh no! And I had hoped that they got rid of him.

Aunt: Who?

Uncle: Mugnog.

Pam: Mugnog said that it'd be better to take a walk now. Then we'll become hungry and can eat a lot of cookies and cake later this afternoon. —That's what Mugnog said.

Uncle: Where is your Mugnog now? (*Looks around him.*)

Tom: He's taking a walk, too. To the mayor's office.

Aunt: To the mayor's office?

Pam: Yeah. And he told us that we should meet him there right away. At city hall.

Uncle: You want to go see the mayor?

Tom: Mugnog's waiting for us there.

Pam: And the mayor, too. (*Softly.*) I hope.

Uncle: The mayor! Well, if that's the case, you shouldn't keep the mayor waiting. Go ahead now, and be careful crossing the streets.

Tom and Pam: Thanks. (*Both exit.*)

Aunt and Uncle eat in silence. After awhile.

Aunt: Tell me, did you mean that?

Uncle: Mean what?

Aunt: Did you really want to let the children go see the mayor because Mugnog's waiting for them there?

Uncle: Naturally. (*Proudly.*) Just imagine: our niece and nephew have been invited to city hall by the mayor.

Aunt: And Mugnog!

Uncle: So what?

Aunt: Well, now you tell me how Mugnog got himself invited to see the mayor?

Uncle: What do you mean?

Aunt: Since when do wooden boxes take walks by themselves? (*Uncle gulps.*) Well?

Uncle (*hits his head with his fist*): Look! Just look at what these children have done to me!! I'm sick. I'm a sick man!

Aunt: Oh, c'mon now. You've just played along.

Uncle: Me? Played along? Joined their stupid game? No—I really believed that Mugnog had taken a walk—I—believed that a wooden box can walk. —Can you imagine that!

Aunt: Don't worry about it.

Uncle: What do you mean, "don't worry about it?" I *am* worried about it. I've got to get my hands on that Mugnog. I've got to kill him!

Aunt: Kill him?

Uncle: Uhhh. I mean—Break it to pieces! Chop it up! Burn it! Bury it!

Aunt: Calm down! Take it easy. Eat something.

Uncle (*stands up*): I've lost my appetite. And it's all his fault— this stupid Mugnog! It's all his fault!

Aunt: Oh, don't be silly. Come and help me clean up.

Uncle: Me? Help you clean up? I'm sick. I'm a sick man. A
   cripple! Mugnog's made me sick. Sick before my time!
Aunt: Well, you make me sick! (*Exits.*)

Mugnogged Again

Uncle: Because of Mugnog, both my
   arms and legs are shaking.
   I'm mugged again! —uh...
   I'm nogged again! —no...

   My head, my heart, my gallstones
   and my guts are aching—
   And worst of all, I know
   it shouldn't scare me.
   The damn thing's just a box,
   It's ordinary...

   Could it be magic? The devil's own?
   It's all the strangest thing I've ever known.

   Holy Mugnog!
   Leave the poor grown-ups, please leave
   the poor grown-ups, please leave
   the poor grown-ups alone.

*The Mayor sits behind a desk. He is writing when the
Policeman appears with Mugnog.*

Policeman: Here you go, Mr. Mayor! (*Places Mugnog on top
   of the desk.*)
Mayor (*without looking up*): What is it?
Policeman: Mugnog.
Mayor: Oh, I see. That's fine. (*Feels Mugnog without looking
   up, suddenly stops, raises his head slowly and stares at
   Mugnog*): What did you say that was?
Policeman: Mugnog!
Mayor: Mind your manners! You think you can pull my leg!

Policeman: No, sir. Not at all, Mr. Mayor.

Mayor: Well, what's this box doing on top of my desk? Take it away!

 Policeman (*takes Mugnog*): I confiscated him.

Mayor: Don't you have anything better to do? Now go out and catch a few thieves, give some parking tickets, or yell at some children and stop them from making noise. But don't come in here again with a confiscated box. A-a-what was that you said? A murdog?

Policeman: Yes, sir. No, sir. Mugnog, sir.

Mayor: Mugnog? —Ridiculous, just ridiculous! I've got no use for ridiculous policemen!

Policeman: But Mr. Schmuck...

Mayor: Cut that out! I'm playing the Mayor now. Can't you see that?

Policeman (*whispers*): That's my next line, dummy!

Mayor: Oh, sorry—Mr. Schmuck is my friend so don't you say anything bad about Mr. Schmuck, you understand?

Policeman: Yes, sir. Just as you say, sir. It's just that Mr. Schmuck wanted me to bring Mugnog—uhh—this box here that I confiscated. He wanted me to deliver it to you personally.

Mayor: Hmmm. —Show it to me. (*The Policeman puts it on the desk again.*) If Mr. Schmuck said that, then—What's inside?

Policeman: Sir! To tell you the truth, I don't know.

Mayor: No?

Policeman: No!

Mayor: Do you think we can...? (*Wants to open the box but is afraid.*) Who does the box belong to?

Policeman: The kids! The two kids who are visiting the Mackepeters.

Mayor: Aha, kids! Can't be anything good. Kids! Always making noise, always loud, poorly behaved. And now they start trouble with this box! Really unbelievable! (*Someone knocks at the door. The Mayor jumps in fright and points at the box.*) Did you hear that? It said something. (*Mayor and Policeman put their ears on either side of Mugnog.*

Someone knocks at the door again. Policeman and Mayor jump and look at each other with startled gazes.) Someone's inside there.

Policeman: Sure must be small! (*Tom and Pam enter.*)

Pam: Can't you even say "come in?"

Mayor (*turns around swiftly*): Oh, so it was you two! What do you want here?

Policeman: It's them. They're the ones.

Mayor: Aha! Then come over here!

Tom (*to Pam*): Oh-oh, we've got another crab on our hands! A real big mouth this time!

Mayor: What was that?

Tom: I said I've got something big in my mouth. I mean I've got to cough to get it out. (*Coughs into a handkerchief.*) There!

Mayor: What kind of a box is this?

Pam: What box?

Mayor: Are you blind or something? This one here!

Tom: But that's no box. That's Mugnog!

Pam: Strange how grown-ups keep saying "box."

Mayor: What's a Mug...?

Tom and Pam (*sing*): A Mugnog's a Mugnog, and we're just us.

Mayor: (*to the Policeman*): Well, patrolman Clubb, you've made my day for me by bringing these two characters here!

Policeman: But Mr. Schmuck, he...

Pam and Tom: ...he's a dumb old fool, at least that's what Mugnog says.

Policeman: What was that???

Mayor: Now you've gone too far with your freshness. Arrest the two of them!

Tom: Hey, we only repeated what Mugnog told us!

Mayor: Damn it all, you little monster! (*Wants to give Tom a slap in the face.*)

Policeman: Stop! You're not allowed to do that!

Mayor: Why not? I'm the Mayor, aren't I? I can do what I

please.

Policeman: Sorry, but even Mayors are not allowed to hit children who don't belong to them—

Pam: ...that's what Mugnog always says.

Policeman: No, Mugnog didn't say that. It's in my law book. (*He pulls out a book and shows it to the Mayor.*) Here!

Mayor: Well, then—then, do something! I can't handle these kids. They're driving me crazy. Go ahead, arrest them already!

Policeman: But on what grounds? They haven't broken any laws.

Mayor: Then get someone here who can handle these two! Get the minister—or the doctor—or the teacher!

Policeman: The teacher. That's a good idea! (*Exits.*)

Tom (*to Pam*): Oh, nooo! A teacher—right in the middle of our vacation!

Mayor: She'll show you a thing or two!

Pam: What's she gonna show us!

Mayor: You know very well: how to obey and...

Tom: But we always obey...

Pam: Almost always.

Tom: We listen to Mugnog all the time.

Mayor: This damned box...

Pam: Do you want us to take him away again?

Tom: Yeah, give him back to us, and then we won't disturb you anymore.

Mayor: I'd really love that, but Mr. Schmuck wanted me to have the box. And afterall, Mr. Schmuck is my friend. And if you two have annoyed him with this box, then I'm going to have to break it to pieces! Like this! (*He pounds rather hard on top of the box so that he hurts his hand.*) Owww! This stinken, no good thing! (*The teacher enters.*)

Pam: Am I seeing things? That's Aunt Molly!

Teacher: Ridiculous. I'm playing the teacher now. Later on I'll be Aunt Molly again.

Mayor: The teacher! Finally. Go ahead, take these two with you. Take them to school and make them write a paper on how to behave and obey.

Teacher: Right in the middle of our vacation? You know I can't do that. The school is closed, and to tell you the truth, I don't even know why you sent for me. It's just plain stupid to make children write papers on how to behave and obey.

Mayor: Then I want you to find out what this Mugnog is.

Teacher: Mugnog?

Tom: He's over there.

Pam: That's our Mugnog!!*Teacher*: Oh, I see. Tell me, who is Mugnog? Looks like a box to me.

Tom: But it's not.

Pam: A Mugnog is a Mugnog.

Teacher: Hmmm, I think I understand.

Mayor: Well, how about telling me?

Teacher: Only children can understand Mugnog. You were a child once, weren't you Mr. Mayor?

Pam: Probably a real pest?

Tom: Yeah, a real louse.

Pam: A stinkpot.

Mayor: I'll let you know that I was a wonderful child: obedient, diligent, and kind.

Pam: How did you let the wonderful child become a horrible mayor?

Teacher: And that's rather dumb of him.

Mayor: Mr. Schmuck...

Pam: Man, is he scared of Mr. Schmuck!

Tom: Scared? Didn't he say they were friends?

Teacher: That's some friendship if he shivers and shakes when Mr. Schmuck is around.

Pam: Haven't you noticed that all grown-ups are scared of one another?

All Grown-ups Are Scared

Tom and Pam (*sing alternately*):

Why are all grown-ups afraid of other grown-ups?

Aunt Molly's scared of patrolman Clubb.
Clubb's afraid of the mayor
who's scared of Mister Schmuck...

Why are all the grown-ups afraid of other grown-ups?
Our Mom's afraid of our snoopy aunt.
Our Dad is frightened by his boss.
Our uncle's scared of his landlord,
And the teacher's scared of the principal.

All grown-ups are afraid.
The poor, poor grown-ups!

Mayor: And why are children scared?
Teacher: Only because grown-ups teach them to be scared.
Pam and Tom:

All grown-ups are afraid of each other
But they're all all-all-all-all-all-all-all-all
afraid of our Mugnog here! (*They laugh.*)

Mayor: I'm not afraid of Mugnog!
Pam: But you are afraid of Mr. Schmuck!
Tom: Just tell Mr. Schmuck that you couldn't do anything
about it, but that we stole Mugnog again. Like this. (*The
children run off with the box.*)
Mayor: Stop! I can't allow that! Do something!
Teacher: Not on your life!
Mayor: But when Mr. Schmuck finds out, he'll stop being my
friend. He'll make trouble for me, and I'll lose my job and
reputation. He won't give me money for my next election
campaign. He'll bring the whole town down on me.
There'll be a scandal. No, I can't afford that. I'd better
disappear for awhile. Leave town. Nobody'll see me if I
run out the back door.
Teacher: Have a good trip, Mr. Mayor.
(*The Mayor exits.*)

Policeman (enters): What was all that noise? Where's the Mayor? And the children, where'd they disappear to?

Teacher: The Mayor's left town, and the children have run off somewhere.

Policeman: With the...?

Teacher: Yes, with Mugnog. And now I'm going, too. (*Exits.*)

Policeman: A catastrophe! The Mayor's left town.

(*The Uncle who is on crutches and Mr. Schmuck enter.*)

Policeman: Oh, there he is again. Good to see you, Mr. Mayor!

Schmuck (falling out of his role): No, dummy, you've got it all wrong again! I'm Mr. Schmuck now. The Mayor's not going to come again. The children drove him away for good.

Policeman (to the Uncle): And who are you?

Uncle: I'm still the Uncle. But now I'm the sick Uncle. Mugnog-sick. Sick of Mugnog!

Policeman (again as policeman): Good afternoon, Mr. Schmuck. Good afternoon, Mr. Mackepeter. What can I do for you?

Mr. Schmuck: We'd like to have a talk with the Mayor.

Policeman: Hmmm, well, the Mayor has—uhh—gone on a trip.

Uncle: What? He's got to do something!

Schmuck: Gone on a trip?! The coward! And I thought he was my friend!

Policeman: What did you expect him to do?

Uncle and Schmuck (pell-mell): Break Mugnog into pieces! Destroy the box! Tear it apart! Burn it! Hack it to pieces!

Policeman: Easy, easy, I don't understand one single word.

Schmuck (points to the Uncle): Just look at this man! He's sick, very sick. Do you know what the cause of his suffering is? Mugnog! (*The Uncle whimpers loudly as soon as he hears the name Mugnog mentioned.*) You see, he can't even hear that word without moaning and groaning. If we dont get rid of this dangerous box soon, then the entire city will become sick. There'll be a Mugnog-epidemic!!

(*Uncle whimpers.*)

Policeman: Gee, I'd like to help, but without the Mayor's permission, my hands are tied. And Mugnog... (*Uncle whimpers*)....Mugnog's in the hands of the kids again. (*Uncle whimpers.*)

Schmuck: So that's how things stand! What sort of a way is that to run a city!! —The Mayor's left town. The police aren't allowed to act. And the children have Mugnog... (*Uncle whimpers*)....and are allowed to run around free. There's only one thing left to do. —

Uncle: I know—give them a good beating!

Schmuck: No, even that won't help us anymore. Only the army can help us now. (*To the Policeman*): Quick, call the General!

Policeman: But isn't that going a bit too far? He certainly won't want to waste his time with Mugnog and...

Uncle: Owwww! Will you stop saying that word!

Schmuck: You can see for yourself how bad things have gotten. Now, go ahead. Call the General.

Policeman (*shrugs his shoulders*): Well, if you think it'll do any good.

Enough

All three: Enough! Enough! Enough!
        Enough! Enough! Enough!
Uncle and Policeman (*continue to sing*): Enough!

Schmuck sings: I've had it up to here.
        They've got to stop
        right now.
        They're gonna pay
        and don't forget it.
        We've tried our best.
        They've failed the test

and now. Too bad.
They're past all hope
squash 'em, whack 'em,
teach 'em respect, respect.
Teach 'em, Teach 'em, Teach 'em!

(*They limp off the stage, and, as they go, they sing*):
Enough, enough, enough!
Enough, enough, enough!

Guitarist (*perhaps as transition to the next scene*):
Why are all the grown-ups afraid of
other grown-ups...

V

(*Pam and Tom with Mugnog*)

Pam: Well, we got away again. What do you want to do now?

Tom: Now we can finally play in peace. The Mayor's left town, and without the Mayor, nobody dares to do a thing against us.

Pam: You're forgetting Mr. Schmuck.

Tom: He's only one person.

Pam: And Uncle Henry?

Tom: Uncle Henry? He can't take Mugnog from us. Aunt Molly won't let him.

Aunt (*with cake and cookies*): What won't I let your Uncle Henry do?

Pam: Take Mugnog from us.

Aunt: You'd better not say that word too loud. When Uncle Henry hears it, he starts acting strange. He thinks he's sick. Mugnog-sick.

Tom: Is that true? Well, we're really sorry.

Aunt: Oh, it's not so bad. I think he's faking most of it. Here's some cake and cookies.

Pam: We like faking and pretending, too.

Aunt: I mean, he's really not that sick. He only wants people to feel sorry for him.

Tom: Where is he? In bed?

Aunt: No, no, it doesn't appear to stop him from getting around. He's gone off somewhere with Mr. Schmuck. —Now go ahead and eat some cake and cookies. If you want some more, just come into the kitchen. (*Exits.*)

Pam: Yummm. It's delicious.

Tom: I really like Aunt Molly. She's a good guy.

(*Uncle and Schmuck sneak on stage.*)

Pam: Why don't you give Mugnog a piece?

(*Uncle whimpers.*)

Tom: What was that?

Pam: Probably Mugnog...(*Uncle whimpers*)...He's hungry.

Tom (*opens the top of Mugnog and throws a cookie inside*): So, now you have a cookie, Mugnog.

(*Uncle whimpers.*)

Pam: He wants more. Here. (*Puts a few more cookies into Mugnog.*) Hope you enjoy them, Mugnog. (*Uncle whimpers.*)

Tom: He's still not satisfied. (*Gives him his last cookie.*) Here you go, you greedy little thing. That was my last one, Mugnog. Honest. (*Uncle whimpers.*)

Pam: Well, how do you like that?! He ate up our cake and cookies. (*Gives Mugnog her last piece of cake.*) Now, that's all there is, Mugnog. (*Uncle whimpers.*)

Tom: He's still hungry. What should we do?

Pam: You'd better run into the kitchen and get some more. But don't say that it's for Mugnog. (*Uncle whimpers. Tom exits. Pam pets Mugnog.*) Don't worry. Tom will be right back with some more.

Schmuck: Now she's alone. Quick, let's go! (*Charges onto the stage with an axe. The Uncle limps right behind him.*) Ha!! Now, we'll destroy him!! (*Lifts the axe.*)

Pam (*frightened*): Help! Tom! Aunt Molly! (*Runs away.*)

Schmuck: So, Mackepeter, now it's all over for Mugnog.

Uncle: Owww! Will you stop saying that name!

Schmuck: Sorry, I mean, now we'll chop this box to pieces!
Uncle: All right, but be careful! Be careful!

Schmuck approaches Mugnog slowly and cautiously. Wants to touch him, but he's afraid. He circles it like a cat about to pounce on its prey but is uncertain how dangerous the prey might be.

Uncle: What's the matter? Something wrong there?
Schmuck: You never know...(*Attempts to scare the box.*) Aha, he's not budging! (*Keeps his distance and wants to hit Mugnog on top with the long end of the axe. Uncle takes cover. Schmuck hits Mugnog softly. Both run away. After awhile they return.*) Nothing happened. (*To the Uncle while handing him the axe.*) How about you trying now?
Uncle (*backs away*): NO!! I'm a sick man! I can't!
Schmuck: Coward!
Uncle: You're afraid yourself!
Schmuck(*looks at the box suspiciously*): You think I'm afraid, huh? Well, I bet you I can do it. (*Approaches more closely.*) I'm not afraid! Not at all. I'm not afraid of anyone. I'm not a coward like you. I'm not...(*Places the edge of the blade on top of Mugnog.*) Ha!—you see? And now—
Schmuck (*lifts the axe very slowly*): And now—
Uncle: And now—
Schmuck (*lifts the axe even higher until he has enough room to strike*): Now! (*The axe comes down and stops right before hitting Mugnog.*)

General: Stop!! (*Schmuck stops in the middle of his swing.*) Have you gone crazy? What'll happen when the bomb explodes?
Uncle and Schmuck: Bomb????
Schmuck: Who are you anyway?
General: The general, of course. Now show some respect!
Uncle and Schmuck (*stand at attention and salute the*

General): Good morning Sir!

General: Good morning, soldiers. At ease! (*They stand at ease.*) Well now, let's discuss the situation here. So that's Mugnog.

Uncle (*almost throws up*): Uaaah!

General: What's the matter with him?

Schmuck: Sir, private Mackepeter is sick!

General: Well, then I can't use him. You're dismissed, private. Go to your barracks. (*Uncle exits.*)

Schmuck: General, that there is Mugnog.

General: Hmm. He's in a bad position for us. Got to get some cannons over there! (*Shows Schmuck where he wants the cannons.*)

Schmuck: Yes, sir! (*Exits.*)

General (*takes out a telescope and observes Mugnog*): Hmmmmm. Holy mackerel! Never seen a weapon like that before! Probably Chinese!

Schmuck (*pulls a cannon onto the stage*): Here you are, General!

General: Aha, the cannon. Set it up!

Schmuck: Yes, sir. Right away, sir! (*He has great difficulty in setting up the cannon, and he eventually points the cannon at the General.*)

General: Hey, hey, private! Watch out with that thing! You want to kill me?

Schmuck: Sorry, General. (*Sets the cannon so that it points in the direction of Mugnog.*)

General: That's good like that. Now the ammunition. I'll go and help you. (*Both exit while Pam and Tom return.*)

Pam: The axe was gigantic. He scared the life out of me!

Tom: That's what I really call playing dirty! (*Looks around him.*) Well, where are they?

Pam: They were just here. (*Looks at the cannon. To the audience*): What's this big thing here?

The children in the audience explain what's what, and who was there.

Tom: Who was here? The General?

Pam: A general! That must have been fun! With a cannon.

Tom: They want to shoot Mugnog. How foolish can you get!?

Pam: Well, what should we do now?

Tom: We've got to hide Mugnog!

Pam: And what should we do with the cannon?

Tom: Let's load it.

Pam: But we don't have any ammunition.

Tom: Yes, we do. The apples over there.

Pam: Good idea! (*They load the cannon with three apples and set it facing the direction of the exit.*)

Tom: Now, quick! We've got to get out of here! (*Takes Mugnog.*) C'mon Mugnog. We've got to hide you. (*Both exit.*)

Aunt (*with her knitting*): Lord oh lord! I'm slowly becoming exhausted. A husband who pretends to be sick and two children who are making the whole town crazy! And a Mugnog who baffles everyone! Lord! (*Sits down on the bench and begins to knit. General and Schmuck enter with ammunition.*)

General (*sees the Aunt and then the cannon which is now aimed at him*): The enemy!!! There! (*Nudges Schmuck, puts the ammunition down and raises his hands in surrender.*)

Schmuck: But that's only...

General: Quick, put your hands up! The enemy's stolen our cannon!

Schmuck (*sets the ammunition on the floor and shrugs his shoulders while raising his hands.*): That's only Mrs. Mackepeter.

Aunt (*looks up and stares in astonishment; she puts her hands up just like the two men and motions them to come over*): Hi! C'mon over here.

General: We surrender. Please don't shoot! Please!

Aunt: Shoot? What should I shoot with?

Schmuck: That's a cannon!

Aunt (*sees the cannon, becomes interested, and examines it*):

That's a cannon? A real cannon? How does it work?
(*Fusses around with it.*)

General: Help! Don't! Please don't! We won't make a move!
We surrender! (*The aunt mistakenly discharges the
cannon. The apples come toppling out. The General and
Schmuck fall down crying.*) "UaaaaH!"

Aunt: Well now, what was that all about? (*Stands up and
discovers the apples.*) My apples! Who put them in the
cannon? (*To the men who are lying on the ground.*) Hey,
are you two sleeping?

General: I'm dead.

Schmuck: Me, too.

Aunt (*laughs*): What a pair of heroes you are!

General (*stands up and tests out his arms and legs*): Hey! I'm
still in one piece. (*To Schmuck*): Soldier, get up from
there. That's no way for a man to act!

Schmuck (*stands up*): And I thought it was all over.
(*Threatens the Aunt with his finger.*) That was a
dangerous thing to do, Mrs. Mackepeter! Don't you ever
scare me like that again!

General (*has cautiously snuck behind the Aunt with a drawn
pistol*): Now I've got you! Put up your hands!

Aunt: Now, now. I've got to finish my knitting. (*Knits.*)

General: But you're my prisoner!

Aunt (*to Schmuck*): Tell me, Mr. Schmuck, who does this
man think he is?

Schmuck: This man you refer to, Mrs. Mackepeter, is none
other but the General!

Aunt (*turns around and sees the pistol. She takes it away from
the General*): A General? Well, I couldn't care if he was
the President. You don't fool around with guns like toys.

General (*to Schmuck*): She's enough to drive me AWOL.

Aunt: Now, don't get fresh! What are you doing in my garden?

Schmuck: We wanted to shoot Mugnog!

Aunt: Oh, come now! Mugnog—this is getting too much for
me to take. A sick husband, a Mayor who's left town, a
city that's gone mad—a Mr. Schmuck who's become a

wild man, a cannon that explodes apples, a General who's
a coward and putters around in our garden—all this
because of Mugnog. This has got to stop. Now, right now.

> Mugnog? Mugnog?
> What's it 'sposed to be?
> Mugnog?! Mugnog?!
> Is it safe to see?
> Things were quiet here, and then—
> Mugnog just comes crashing in.
> Far and near,
> all we hear
> till it's coming
> out our ears.
> Mugnog!

Schmuck: Bravo!

Aunt: Oh, be quiet!

General : Do you mind if I have my pistol back? (*Wants to take the pistol from her.*)

Aunt: This is not a toy, General. I'm going to throw it away—and your stupid cannon as well.

General: This is treason! I'm going to tell the President about this! (*Exits.*)

Aunt (*to Schmuck*): What are you standing around for? Get out of here!

Schmuck: I only want to help you destroy Mugnog. That's all.

Aunt: I'll take care of Mugnog myself. I don't need your help. Now get out of here! (*Schmuck exits. As he leaves, he takes an apple and secretly sticks it into his pocket.*) Well, it's time to clean up around here. Pam! Tom!

Pam and Tom: Yes, Aunt Molly!

Aunt: Come and help me throw this junk into the garbage cans. (*Pam and Tom sing while they help: The Mugnog song. Tom carries off the cannon and the pistol.*)

Pam: Where are...

Aunt: The General and Mr. Schmuck? I sent them away.

Pam: You're really brave, Aunt Molly.

Aunt: What do you mean brave? Those two men are the world's worst cowards.

Pam: Hey, that's really good—the world's worst cowards. That's what Mugnog would say, too!

Aunt: That reminds me. We've got to have a little talk about your Mugnog. Things can't go on like this much longer.

Pam: Oh-oh, now she's starting in. (*Both exit.*)

VI

Mugnog is under a stool. Pam comes and spreads a table cloth over the stool so that Mugnog cannot be seen. Tom follows her.

Pam: Well, how does that look?

Tom: I'm not sure whether that's going to be enough.

Pam: Sure it will. Nobody'll look for him there.

Tom: Let's hope so. (*The door bell rings.*)

Pam: You get it.

Tom: I'd rather not. It's got to be someone who wants to get rid of Mugnog. (*The doorbell rings again.*)

Pam: Okay, let him wait outside.

Aunt: Isn't anyone going to get it? (*Runs to the door.*)

Tom: Did it ring?

Aunt: Now, don't pretend that you didn't hear! (*Opens the door. The Policeman enters.*)

Pam: Who's he supposed to be now? A General or a Doorman?

Tom: Maybe he's the TV Man?

Policeman: I'm patrolman Clubb.

Pam: Then it's okay. If you were the General, we'd throw you right out.

Aunt: Officer Clubb, what is it you want now?

Policeman: I want Mugnog. Orders from the President's Assistant!

All the others: The President's Assistant!!!

Policeman: That's right! Just think! (*Proudly.*) The Assistant is sitting in the Mayor's office and wants to see Mugnog!

Tom: If he wants to see Mugnog, then he'll have to come here.

Pam: Mugnog's had enough walks for today. He doesn't want to go out anymore.

Aunt: All right, now stop this. Once and for all. This game has got to end. You've made the entire city crazy with your Mugnog. Uncle Henry is so sick that I've had to call the doctor...

Doctor (*entering*): He's really not that sick, Mrs. Mackepeter.

Aunt: Oh, Doctor. Tell me, how is he?

Doctor: Your husband's fine. There's nothing wrong with him. He's a little moody. Just be nice to him and pretend he's sick. That's what he wants. And remember not to say Mugnog in front of him. Otherwise he'll become nervous.

Policeman: The whole city's nervous because of this Mugnog.

Doctor: That's ridiculous. Let the children play and enjoy themselves.

Policeman: I'm sorry. I can't allow that. The President's Assistant wants to see Mugnog.

Doctor: Did I hear you right? —Did you say the President's Assistant?

Pam (*to the Doctor*): Just imagine, Doctor, the President's Assistant is sitting in the Mayor's office waiting for Mugnog.

Tom: Well, let him wait!

Aunt: What's so important about the President's Assistant anyway?

Pam: He's probably just another one of those snoops snooping around! (*The Assistant enters.*)

Policeman (*with respect*): It's the President's Assistant! —Sir!

Pam: You see. Just like I said!

Tom: Snoop! Snoop! Snoop!

Aunt: Will you be quiet! Excuse me, sir, but my nephew is sometimes quite fresh.

Assistant: I can see that. The brat! (*To the policeman*): Tell me, officer, how long did you expect me to wait at city hall. I have many important things to take care of.

Pam: Don't believe him! (*Doctor laughs.*)

Policeman: Doctor!

Assistant: Where is this—this—

Doctor, Aunt, Policeman: Mugnog??

Assistant: Yes, this Mugnog!

Aunt (*looks around*): He must be somewhere around here. C'mon you two, show us where you've hidden him.

Pam: He hid himself. (*Sits down on the stool.*)

Tom: And he's not going to tell us where. (*He sits down next to Pam.*)

Assistant (*to the policeman*): Well, get a move on. What are you standing there for? Go look for it! (*To the Aunt and the Doctor*): And you, too. Get going! Get going! I'll conduct the search. (*They all look for Mugnog. The Policeman crawls on the floor. The Doctor pretends to look. The Aunt becomes slightly hysterical and cries out: "My rugs, my furniture, my antiques, etc." Tom and Pam sit close together on the stool. The Assistant pokes around with his walking cane and lifts the table cloth.*)

Searching Song

Policeman: I see him here!

Assistant: I feel him here—

Aunt: I hear him here—
   I'll eat my hat
   if this makes any sense to me!

Policeman: I hear it here!

Assistant: I hear it there!

Policeman: I think I'll call the squad cars
   in from precinct three.

Assistant: This Mugnog can't escape.
   I swear I'll find him.

Policeman: And you can count on me.
    I'm right behind him!
Pam: They're awful loud!
Tom: What? I couldn't hear!
Aunt: I think that
    Mugnog's hiding
    very near.
Policeman and Assistant: I think that
    Mugnog's somewhere
    very near.

Assistant: Ahaa! I think I've got him!
Doctor (*quickly*): Really? Let me see! (*Leans over the stool, takes Mugnog into his hands, and hides him behind his back.*) Nothing there. You'd better keep looking.
Pam: Whaaa?
Doctor: Shhh. (*Sneaks slowly to the door.*)
Assistant: I felt for sure that was him! There was something there!
Tom: That was my leg, snoop!
Policeman: You want me to arrest him, sir?
Assistant (*watches the Doctor*): Arrest him? Yes, go ahead, but that one there! (*Points to the Doctor.*)
Aunt: The Doctor?
Policeman: The Doctor?
Assistant: That's right. The Doctor! Turn him around and look at what he's got!
The Doctor turns himself around and attempts to conceal Mugnog.
Policeman: So, something was there afterall. (*Moves to the Doctor and tears Mugnog from him.*)
All: Mugnog!
Assistant: Bring him to me, Officer!
Doctor (*to the children*): Sorry about that.
Tom: That's all right.
Pam: It's just an old wooden box.
Aunt: What did you say?
Policeman: She said, a wooden box.

Assistant: I thought it was the Mugnog.

Tom: How dumb can you be! Mugnog—what's that supposed to be?

Pam: Anyone can see that's just a plain old wooden box.

Assistant (*to the Policeman*): Open it up!

Policeman (*is afraid*): I-uhhh—I think something's in there.

Assistant: Ahaa! Then hand it over to me. (*Places the box on the table, touches the top.*)

Policeman: Careful! (*Takes cover while the others follow his example. Assistant stands back and opens the top with his cane. Then he slowly moves closer and looks inside.*)

Assistant: Aaah! Cookies and cake! (*He reaches inside, takes a cookie, and begins to eat it.*) Hmmm! Delicious! Here, try one. (*He hands the Policeman a cookie.*)

Pam: Now they're even eating up our cookies.

Tom: That's typical for President's assistants. They'll rob anything they can get their hands on!

Aunt (*proudly to the Assistant*): I baked them myself.

Assistant: You have my compliments, my dear lady. Pack up the rest for my trip back to Washington. I've got to be off. I enjoyed my stay immensely. (*Aunt gets a bag for the cookies and gives it to him.*) Well, I've done my job! Good bye, everyone!

Doctor: Don't you want to arrest me?

Assistant: What for? There were only these cookies inside. (*Exits.*)

Doctor: Then I might as well go, too. Take care of yourselves, and don't bother your uncle so much. (*Exits.*)

Policeman: I don't understand. Everyone's going away now, and Mugnog's staying here. What should I do with him?

Aunt: I think you should just leave him here.

Pam: Oh, let him take it.

Tom: What do we want with a plain old wooden box?

Aunt: But, but—now cut this out! Stop pretending that you don't care. It's your Mugnog!

Uncle (*enters wearing a bathrobe*): No! Please don't, I can't stand that word! Oww! Oww! (*Notices the Policeman.*) What's the TV Man doing here?

Policeman: First of all, I'm Patrolman Clubb, and second of all I'm not staying in this crazy house any longer. I'm leaving. This is a real madhouse! (*Exits.*)

Aunt: How rude!

Pam: He's really fresh!

Tom: No manners!

Uncle: Will you quit yelling! You know that I'm a...(*The doorbell rings.*)

They all sigh: Mr. Schmuck!! (*Aunt lets him in.*)

Schmuck: What's all the noise about? (*Looks at the box.*) Ahaa, there's the—

Uncle: Nooo!

Schmuck: The thing—the blob—the box! (*Goes to the box and wants to grab it. He turns around to see if someone is going to stop him. Pounds on the box with a "Ha!" Waits a second and then pounds on the top again: "Ha!" Finally, he takes the box from the table.*)

Pam (to Tom): C'mon. Let's go. This is getting boring. (*Exit.*)

Schmuck: Finally! Now we can do what we want with it. (*Begins to take the box apart.*)

Uncle: This is great!

Aunt: Great? I think it's mean. The Mugnog box belongs to the children! Give it to me. (*She runs over to Schmuck, who evades her and, after a brief chase, runs out of the room.*) He's just plain mean and cruel! — The poor children!

Uncle: The children! Of course, you never think about your poor husband!

Aunt: Oh, you—(*behind the scene there is a loud chopping and sawing noise.*) What's that?

Uncle: Hehehe! That's Mr. Schmuck. He's smashing the thing to smithereens! Haha, I'm beginning to feel better. In fact, I almost feel completely healthy again.

Aunt: Poor Mugnog.

Uncle: Go ahead. You can say *Mugnog* again. I don't mind. Doesn't disturb me in the least. Mugnog's dead! Haha! (*Jumps with glee in the air.*)

The doorbell rings. Aunt opens it.

Schmuck: Here, Mrs. Mackepeter. You wanted to have the
Mugnog back. Now you have him! Ha, ha, ha! (*Dumps
the remains of Mugnog on the floor.*)

Aunt: Oh now! You're terrible! Tom! Pam!

*In the meantime the Uncle thanks Mr. Schmuck. Tom and
Pam appear. Pam is carrying an old, funny-looking stove-pipe
under her arm.*

Tom: What's the matter, Aunt Molly?

Aunt (*points to the floor*): There! It's Mugnog!

Tom: But that's not Mugnog! That's just some wood.

*Pam turns to look, and as she does, she accidentally hits
Schmuck in the stomach with the stove-pipe.*

Schmuck: Hey, watch what you're doing with that miserable
stove-pipe!

Pam and Tom: Stove-pipe???

Aunt: Where'd you find it?

Tom: What?

Uncle: The pipe!

Pam: That's no pipe. That's—

Pam and Tom: Mugnog!

All the others (*begin to moan loudly*): No, no. That can't be
true! It's beginning all over again!

Schmuck: Help! Police! Help!

*Policeman comes running into the room. Schmuck grabs him
and points with horror at the stove-pipe.*

Schmuck: There! There! Do you see it?

Policeman: The pipe?

Schmuck: That's no pipe, that's—

Everyone: Mugnog!

Schmuck: Quick! Arrest him!

Policeman: No. No and no! I'm not going to have anything
more to do with Mugnogs. I've already suffered enough.

Schmuck: Then I'm gonna destroy it myself. I'm gonna
destroy all the Mugnogs in the world! (*Takes the*

stove-pipe which consists of five parts. He begins pulling on the pipes. When he pulls the first part and puts it on the table, the aunt speaks.

Aunt: Now we have two Mugnogs! (*Schmuck puts another part on the table.*)

Pam: Three Mugnogs!! (*Schmuck puts another part on the table.*)

Tom: Four Mugnogs!! (*Schmuck puts the last part on the table.*)

Uncle: Five Mugnogs!!

Pam: Wow! Did I hear you right, Uncle Henry?? Did you say *Mugnog*??

Tom: I think he's finally learned.

Schmuck (*to Uncle*): Are you sure that all these things are Mugnogs?

Uncle: You can see for yourself—that's what Mugnog always says.

Schmuck: Mackepeter, I demand an explanation! What's all this funny business!?

Uncle: Stop yelling at me! —That's what Mugnog says.

Policeman: You want me to arrest him?

Schmuck: You keep out of this! I've got enough problems!

Uncle: And stop bossing officer Clubb around. That's what Mugnog says.

Schmuck (*takes a deep breath but is afraid to explode*): But—but—

Policeman: But you're talking to Mr. Schmuck.

Uncle: Mr. Schmuck is a real schmuck. That's what Mugnog says. He has no business ordering people around in our house, and if he does, out he goes. —That's what Mugnog says.

Aunt: I think we should leave him alone, Henry. He hasn't learned yet.

Pam: Yeah. He's still too little.

Tom: But we shouldn't give up hope. He can still grow up and learn.

All: That's what Mugnog says.

Schmuck: Now I've had—

Enough

All sing alternately with the exception of Schmuck and the Policeman.

      Enough, enough, enough!
      Enough, enough, enough!

Tom: This isn't fun anymore.

Pam: You're too dumb for us.

Uncle: Some people never learn.

Aunt: Down with the sourpusses!

Tom and Pam: But if you want,
      you can find your own
      Mugnogs and play at home.

Tom, Pam, Aunt and Uncle:
      Now Mugnog's tired out and wants to go.
      We're finished with the play.
      The time has come to say.
      We're finished with the play,
      the time has come to say:
      Enough, enough, enough!
      Enough, enough, enough!
      —That's what Mugnog says!

SONGS FROM:
"MUGNOG"

MUGNOG

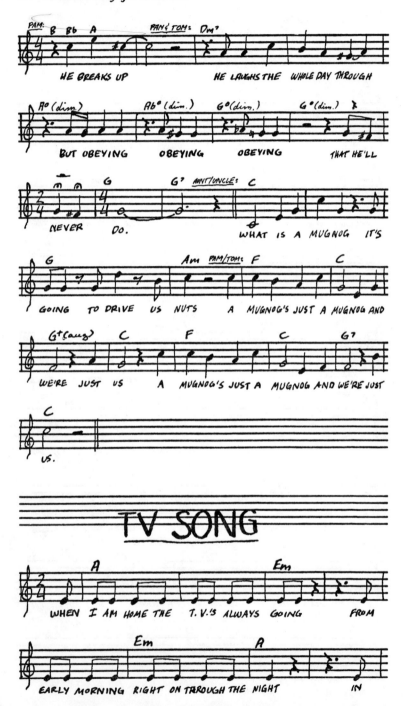

HE BREAKS UP   HE LAUGHS THE WHOLE DAY THROUGH

BUT OBEYING   OBEYING   OBEYING   THAT HE'LL

NEVER   DO.   WHAT IS A MUGNOG   IT'S

GOING   TO DRIVE   US   NUTS   A MUGNOG'S JUST A MUGNOG AND

WE'RE   JUST   US   A MUGNOG'S JUST A MUGNOG AND WE'RE JUST

US.

TV SONG

WHEN I AM HOME THE   T.V.'S ALWAYS GOING   FROM

EARLY MORNING RIGHT ON THROUGH THE NIGHT   IN

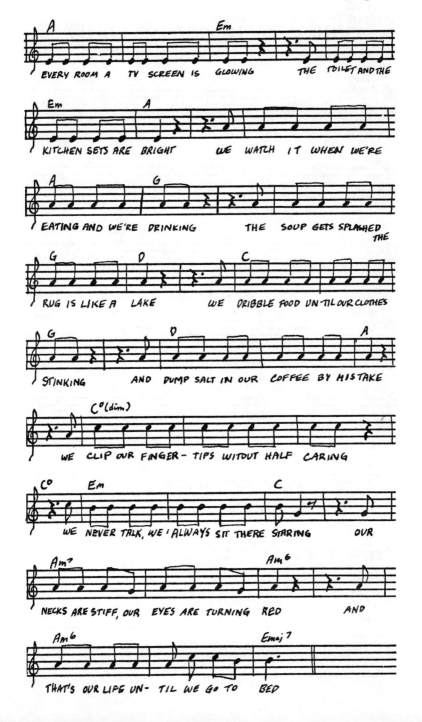

THEY'RE MUCH TOO LOUD

GARDEN SONG

MUGNOGGED AGAIN

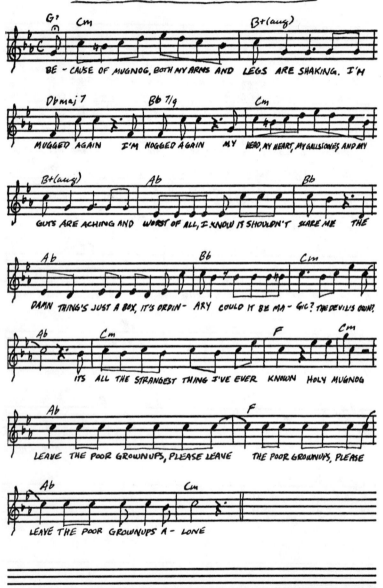

WHY ARE GROWNUPS SCARED

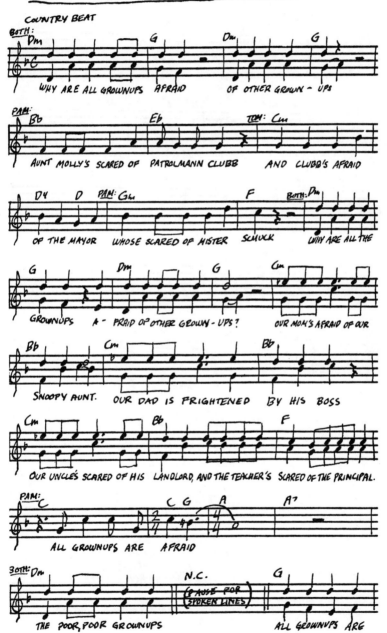

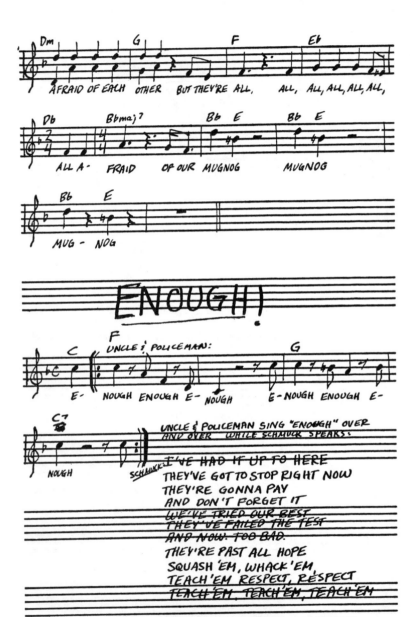

AFRAID OF EACH OTHER BUT THEY'RE ALL, ALL, ALL, ALL, ALL, ALL,

ALL A- FRAID OF OUR MUGNOG MUGNOG

MUG - NOG

ENOUGH!

UNCLE & POLICEMAN:

E- NOUGH ENOUGH E- NOUGH E-NOUGH ENOUGH E-

NOUGH SCHMUCK:

UNCLE & POLICEMAN SING "ENOUGH" OVER
AND OVER WHILE SCHMUCK SPEAKS:

I'VE HAD IT UP TO HERE
THEY'VE GOT TO STOP RIGHT NOW
THEY'RE GONNA PAY
AND DON'T FORGET IT
WE'VE TRIED OUR BEST
THEY'VE FAILED THE TEST
AND NOW. TOO BAD.
THEY'RE PAST ALL HOPE
SQUASH 'EM, WHACK 'EM
TEACH 'EM RESPECT, RESPECT
TEACH 'EM. TEACH 'EM, TEACH 'EM

UNCLE, POLICEMAN, AND SCHMUCK SING "ENOUGH" AFTER
SCHMUCK FINISHES SPEAKING.

SEARCHING SONG

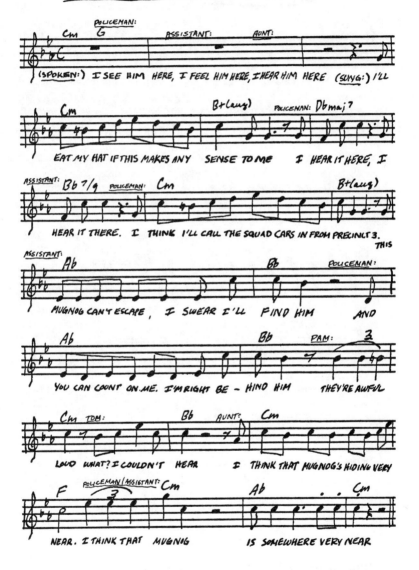

(SPOKEN:) I SEE HIM HERE, I FEEL HIM HERE, I HEAR HIM HERE (SUNG:) I'LL

EAT MY HAT IF THIS MAKES ANY SENSE TO ME I HEAR IT HERE, I

HEAR IT THERE. I THINK I'LL CALL THE SQUAD CARS IN FROM PRECINCT 3.
THIS

MUGNOG CAN'T ESCAPE, I SWEAR I'LL FIND HIM AND

YOU CAN COUNT ON ME. I'M RIGHT BE - HIND HIM THEY'RE AWFUL

LOUD WHAT? I COULDN'T HEAR I THINK THAT MUGNOG'S HIDING VERY

NEAR. I THINK THAT MUGNOG IS SOMEWHERE VERY NEAR

ENOUGH (FINALE)

THE SONGS IN "MUGNOG" WERE WRITTEN BY:
WORDS: VOLKER LUDWIG ; MUSIC: BIRBER HEYMANN ; TRANSLATED
FROM ORIGINAL GERMAN: JACK ZIPES ; MUSIC ADAPTED: ANNE WARREN

BIZZY, DIZZY, DAFFY

AND ARTHUR

Original title: *Balle, Malle, Hupe und Artur* by Dagmar Dorsten, Uli Gressieker, Volker Ludwig, Stefan Ostertag, Carsten Krüger and the premiere cast. English translation by Jack Zipes.

Characters:

Bizzy
Dizzy
Daffy
Arthur
Knick
Knock
Voices on Tape

Prologue

Bizzy (comes on stage and whistles through a tea kettle top which she has on a string around her neck): Dizzy! Daffy! —C'mon out! (*Whistles a signal.*)

Dizzy (answers from backstage with the same signal on a bicycle bell, runs back and forth, and then appears on stage): Hey, where's Daffy keeping himself?

Bizzy: Funny... (*To audience*): Have you seen him?

Dizzy: He's got hair *this* long—

Bizzy: Wrong, dummy, it's *this* long—

Dizzy: ...and he grins and honks all day long.

Bizzy: Maybe he'll come if we all call him together.

Dizzy: Let's try.

Bizzy: One, two, three!

All: Daaafeee!!

Dizzy: That's not the way. I'll show you how to do it. Now quiet, everybody! (*She rings her bell, and Bizzy whistles until Daffy, who has been sitting in the audience, honks back.*)

Bizzy: Do you see him? (*The audience recognizes him.*)

Dizzy: No, where is he? (*The audience informs Dizzy.*) Ah, there he is! Hey, Daffy, c'mon over here!

Daffy: Not today, Mrs. Beanpole! It's much nicer over here!

Bizzy: How come?

Daffy: Because the sun's shining here, and where you are it's raining and—(*he turns to the audience and holds his nose*)—it stinks!

Dizzy: Then I'll let you have my umbrella. (*Pretends she has an umbrella.*)

Daffy: Yeah, but your lousy umbrella has a hole in it where the stink goes through!

Bizzy (examines the imaginary umbrella): Well, what do you know about that? You're right. The umbrella does have a hole in it.

Dizzy: Damned umbrella! (*Throws it away.*) C'mon over here anyway. Rain's good for you. Helps you grow big and strong!

Daffy: Not me. Rain always makes me shrink! Only frogs like you like rain!

Bizzy (lets Dizzy push her): Ow! Ow! My foot! Owww! Oooh! (*Begins to limp.*)

Daffy (rushes over to her): Hey, what's going on? What's wrong with your foot?

Bizzy (jumps around as soon as Daffy is on stage): Haha! You fell for it! Sucker!

Daffy: Then—then, it was all just a lie about your foot!

Dizzy: No, not really. Just a little trick so that you'd come over here.

Daffy: It was too a lie!

Bizzy: No, just a trick. That's allowed.

Daffy: And I'm telling you it was a lie, a plain old lousy lie!

Bizzy and Dizzy: And we're telling you it was just a trick, a good old trick!

They banter back and forth a few times.

Daffy (to audience): It was too a lie about her foot, wasn't it?

Dizzy: Well? Was it a lie or just a trick?

They take part in the debate in the audience making sounds and noise.

Daffy: All right, it was a trick! (*They all sound their noisemakers.*)

Dizzy (begins to talk while the other two take seats on the garbage can): Hey, cut the clowning, you two! I guess it's about time to tell you who we are. You see, we three, Bizzy, Dizzy, and Daffy, all live on the same street.

Bizzy: On Garbage Can Street! (*Pushes Daffy off the can.*)

Daffy: I live at Number One Garbage Can Street. —Ow, my knee. You broke it!

Bizzy: Hey, I'm sorry. I didn't mean to push you so hard. (*Springs off the can.*)

Daffy (jumps quickly back on the can): Thanks, that was just a little trick so that I could get a better seat on the can. (*Lets Bizzy sit next to him.*)

Dizzy: On Garbage Can Street there are 99 dogs—

Daffy (in a low voice): Bow wow! (*Growls.*)

Dizzy: 50 of them are these little Beagles—

Daffy (in a high voice): Woo-woo! (*Growls.*)

Daffy: Then there are 22 streetlamps and fire hydrants which the dogs always pee on—

Bizzy: —and no playground.

Daffy: But there are over a 100 cars, all with horns— (*He honks.*)

Dizzy: 2 mailboxes, a chewing gum machine that Daffy broke, and a pay telephone that never works—

Bizzy: —and no playground.

Daffy: But 33 grumpy old people always complaining—

Bizzy: —and one Mr. Tease. (*Points at Daffy.*)

Daffy: —and one Miss Tease! (*Points at Bizzy.*)

Bizzy: And one beanpole!

Dizzy: And one split pea! (*From now on, faster and more rhythmically.*)

Bizzy: And because there's no playground here—

Dizzy: And because our parents are always away the whole day—

Daffy: And because people are always yelling at us—

All: —we've formed our own group.

Bizzy: And whoever does anything against Dizzy or Daffy—

Daffy: Or against Bizzy and Dizzy—

Dizzy: Or against Bizzy and Daffy—

All: —has to deal with us!

(*They all break into the song.*)

Just One Is No One

All: Bizzy, Dizzy, Daffy
began one day to moan:
There's nothing doing home
and I am all alone.
My parents don't have time to play.
The playground's much too far away.

Daffy: Just one is no one.

All: Two can get much more done.
　　　They shove us and leave us like crumbs.
　　　To stay alone is just no fun!
Bizzy: Just one is no one.
All: Two can get much more done.
　　　And if the two should grow to three,
　　　The rest will join, you wait and see!
Dizzy: Just one is no one.
All: Two can get much more done.
　　　The grown-ups tell us what to do.
　　　They still boss us around.
　　　But soon we will be more and more,
　　　then watch us go to town!

Daffy: Damn, I've got to go now...Got to do my homework.
Dizzy: Wait a second. I'll come with you and help you out.
　　　Two can work faster than one.
Bizzy: And I'll copy what you do today, and tomorrow you can
　　　copy from me.
Daffy: That's a deal. We'll see you later.
Dizzy: Yeah, meet us here at the garbage can.
Bizzy: O.K. I'll be waiting here for you.
(*Dizzy and Daffy leave.*)

*Bizzy looks up and down the street and then at the audience
while humming a song. She takes numerous objects out of her
pants pocket, opens the garbage can, throws a few things in,
takes other things out, finally fishes out an old, dried-out
paint brush, spits on it, tries to paint on the house wall, ends
up playing airplane and imitating jet noises with her mouth
and whistles.*
*Authur comes on stage slowly. He doesn't see Bizzy right away
but then notices her. When she looks at him, he avoids her
glance. Bizzy teases him with her brush. Finally he comes
closer.*
Arthur: Hey, —uh—what you doin' there?
Bizzy: I'm flying. (*Continues to play airplane and attracts his
　　　attention.*) Who're you?

Arthur: None of your business!

Bizzy (*to audience*): Any of you know him?—I don't either. (*Continues playing.*)

Arthur: Flying? Where to? The moon?

Bizzy: No, dummy. To China. The moon's up there.

Arthur: Why China?

Bizzy: Don't you ever watch tv?

Arthur: Of course I watch tv!

Bizzy: Well, aren't you interested in what they're doing there?

Arthur: Of course, I am.

Bizzy: Hey you better watch out!

Arthur: What for?

Bizzy: Because the ocean's there, dummy! Right there where you're standing. You'd better start swimming!

Arthur: You mean I'm standing in the ocean?

Bizzy: Don't you even know geography? Here's America— there's China—and the ocean's in the middle. You got to swim, and you better do it fast! —What a nincompoop! Stands in the middle of the ocean and can't even swim!

Arthur: I've never seen such a stupid game!

Bizzy: Go on, swim! If you don't, you're gonna drown!

Arthur: Oh, all right: I'm swimming. —Have I reached land yet?

Bizzy: Of course. Can't you even tell the difference between land and water?

Arthur: Do you know what you are! A—a puny old piper cub flier.

Bizzy: Geez, you're dumber than I thought! Can't you tell a supersonic jet when you see one?

Arthur: You mean a supersonic paintbrush! —Girls don't even know what a supersonic jet is.

Bizzy: Oh yeah? Well now I'm flying at three times the speed of sound—Sss ssss. Boom!

(*Arthur tries in vain to take the brush away.*)

Arthur: Come on, let me have a turn!

Bizzy: Sure. (*Gives him the paintbrush.*)

Arthur (*plays without enthusiasm and throws the brush away*): Hey, listen. I've got an idea. Let's pretend that the airplane has crashed. I'll be the pilot, and I'm going to crash. (*Crashes.*)

Bizzy: And I'll be Robinson Crusoe on the island, and I see you crash.

Arthur: No. It doesn't go like that. You're the coast guard, and you come with a stretcher and pull me out.

Bizzy: A stretcher, in the middle of the ocean?...No, I'm Robinson Crusoe, and I come with my canoe and pull you out.

Arthur: But you got to play the coast guard!

Bizzy: Why?

Arthur: Because I said so!

Bizzy: Who d'you think you are, the big boss or something? I'll play whatever *I* want and not what you tell me to play!

Arthur: No, you can't!

Bizzy: Why not?

Arthur: Because you've got no brains!

Bizzy: You're the one who's got no brains. No one could play with you. You'd drive everyone crazy.

Arthur: You dumb cluck! You don't even know what you're talking about! You're dumber than my sister, and she's pretty dumb when you get right down to it!

Complaining lady (*who yells from a nearby window*): Quiet out there!! I told you once, and I'm telling you again: keep out of here! This used to be a quiet place, and now you little brats are taking over! Just wait till I tell your parents! Just wait till they get home from work! I'll give them a piece of my mind, and then they'll let you have it. Now, scram! (*She slams the window shut. Arthur has disappeared. He hides behind the garbage can.*)

Bizzy (*has pressed herself flat against the house wall, yawns affectedly, holds her ears shut, mimics the lady, and giggles*): Never fails. No matter where we play, someone always nags at us...Hey, where's that dopey pilot! Did he run away?

Arthur (*comes out of his hiding place*): Hey, here I am. —C'mon, let's play somewhere else.

Bizzy: My name's not hey. My name's Robinson Crusoe, and I
have to stay on my island. —Say, what's *your* name,
anyway?

Arthur: None of your business.

Bizzy: You know what you are, a real creep! As far as I'm
concerned, you can play by yourself. So long...

Arthur (*upset*): My name's Arthur, Arthur...Arthur, the
famous pirate, and I know a real good game...I'm
shipwrecked, and you can be Robinson Crusoe and save
me..."Help! I'm drowning!!" (*Struggles with swimming
motions, and she plays as though she's pulling him out
with a rope.*)

Bizzy: Hold on! I'm coming!!

Arthur: Help! Help!

Complaining Lady: You damned brats!! Cut that noise out!!

(*Arthur runs away, completely frightened. Bizzy hides.*)
Someone should put you behind bars, and your parents,
too! Clear out, or I'll call the police. Just wait, I'm gonna
come down and let you have it! (*Window slams shut.*)

Bizzy (*right before fleeing*): That's what I call being a good
neighbor! She probably ate a rotten egg for breakfast.
(*Exits.*)

II

*In front of another house. Bizzy on stage, followed by Arthur
in the distance. He stays in the background. Dizzy and Daffy
signal each other from the backstage. Then they appear on
stage.*

Daffy: So there you are!

Dizzy: Why didn't you meet us at the garbage can?

Bizzy: Well, uh—well—

Daffy: You just left, huh?

Bizzy: No—I mean—yes, but...

Dizzy: What're you trying to say?

Daffy: Bizzy's took a spin, and now she's in a tizzy.

Bizzy: Cut that out! —It was like this: I was playing by the garbage can, minding my own business, and along comes this guy, and his name is Ar-thur...You can't imagine how goofy this kid is. Real impossible. Always trying to get his own way.

Daffy: Oh no! What a creep!

Dizzy: And where's he now?

Bizzy: No idea. The way that old hag yelled at us—

Daffy: Again?

Bizzy: Yup, and he got so scared that he took off faster than a jet. You should've seen him go! And I ran away last because I wasn't as scared as he...

Arthur (who in the meantime has come up to them): Don't believe a word she says!

Dizzy: Is that Arthur?

Bizzy (nods): Don't try and say you didn't run away from that old hag!

Arthur: I didn't. I just thought I heard my mother calling me!

Daffy: Oh yeah?! Do you always run home *right* away?

Arthur: I—I thought is was time to eat. And I was pretty hungry.

Dizzy: But it's already way past lunch time!

Arthur: I thought it was dinner time already.

Daffy: It's much too early for dinner.

Arthur: Well, I—I really thought—that the woman would hit us.

Daffy: Hit you...! When there were two of you? There's no need to be afraid *then*!

Bizzy: He's just dumb.

Daffy: He can't help it.

Bizzy: And besides, his name's Ar-thur.

Daffy: He can't help that either. His parents gave him that name.

Bizzy: Still...

Daffy: Listen, Bizzy, we *need* more guys in our group! Then people won't be able to chase us away so easily.

Bizzy: More guys maybe—but no Arthurs!

Daffy: Oh, c'mon. Why not? At least we could give him a

chance.

Bizzy: I don't know.

Dizzy: We'll give him one more chance. O.K.? Now, let's play
something. (*To Arthur*): What do you want to play?

Daffy (*since Arthur can't think of anything*): I know! Moon
landing!

Arthur: Oh boy! Just like on tv! I'll play the first man to walk
on the moon.

Bizzy (*mimics him*): "I'll play the first man to walk on the
moon."

Daffy: And I'll float around you in the space capsule or look at
a few stars in the meantime.

Arthur: No, that's all wrong. You're my crew!

Bizzy: I'd rather play someone from another planet!

Arthur: There isn't any such stupid thing!

Bizzy: How do you know, smarty? You wait and see!

Dizzy (*to Arthur*): Oh, let her play what she wants...

Arthur (*with contempt*): She can go jump in the lake as far as
I'm concerned...

Dizzy: O.K. You two are creatures from outerspace, and we're
both from the earth.

(*Bizzy and Daffy hide. Arthur and Dizzy play moonlanding.*)

Arthur: Stop! I get out first! I'm the captain!... Well, it's
pretty dusty out here on the moon.

Dizzy: Just look at the way the earth shines! There!

Arthur: What did you say?

Dizzy: When we're on the earth, the moon shines. So now
we're on the moon, and the earth's shining. Don't you see
it?

Arthur: Noo!

Dizzy: Oh, forget it!...Hey look, we can hop around.
Nothing's holding us down!! (*Hops.*)

Daffy (*carries Bizzy on his shoulders, and they move their arms
in rhythm*): O.K., here we come!

Arthur: What're they supposed to be?

Dizzy: Hey, look, a moon giraffe! How's it going, moon
giraffe? I'm lieutenant Dizzy from the earth. (*Shakes
Bizzy's hand first. Confusion because of the four hands.*

Arthur hits the giraffe on the paw.) Hey! You crazy? It's a
friendly animal. Go on, keep playing.

Arthur: Get away from our spaceship, or we'll shoot you with
our ray guns! (*Shoots.*) Bang! Bang!

Bizzy: Cut it out! He's ruining the whole game with his stupid
guns! You turkey!

Arthur: *You're* the turkey! Martians are supposed to be
enemies.

Bizzy: How do you know we're Martians? And who says
Martians are enemies?

Daffy: Forget it, it was only a game. . .

Arthur: Moon landing was stupid anyway. I know something
much better. Cops and robbers. I'll play the police chief.

Daffy, Bizzy, and Dizzy: Naturally. . .

Arthur: . . .and you're (*to Daffy*) the robber. You two (*to
Bizzy and Dizzy*) are the cops, and you bring him to me.
(*Bizzy and Dizzy take Daffy between them and lead him in
while having a lot of fun with the game.*) Name?!

Daffy: Arthur.

Arthur: Ridiculous.

Daffy: It's not ridiculous. My name's Arthur Crackpot, and
I'm a robber. And what's your name, Chief?

Arthur: None of your business! So you've pulled off another
one of your famous jobs.

Daffy: Damned right I have, and I had a great time. You
should try it yourself, Chief. Last night I snuck into a
bakery, and there were thousands of cookies and cakes
there!

Arthur: Aha!

Daffy: Boy, did we eat!

Arthur: What do you mean "we"?

Daffy: Uh—uh, me and the two cops here! —Would you like a
taste? I think I got some leftovers in my pocket.

Arthur: What was that? You broke in, too? That's the worst
thing a cop can do! You're both fired!

Daffy: C'mon, Chief, let's go break into our school and steal
all the report cards! (*The girls giggle loudly.*)

Arthur: Boy, I'm not gonna play anymore! I don't know of any

robbers like the one you're playing! And cops who laugh
like dumb clucks! —You don't know anything! And anyway, girls are always ruining games. The only thing they
know how to do is giggle!

Dizzy: Arthur, you're a real fink, aren't you?

Arthur: You're the fink! You're such a fink that you don't even
know what a fink is! Finks!

Voice of a neighbor: What's all that noise out there? You're
not allowed to play here. I've told you a hundred times!
Now go play somewhere else! If I catch you just one more
time. . .

Old lady: I don't know what's getting into these children!
Don't they know how to play quietly?

Voice of a neighbor: Just get 'em out of here!

(*The three children take the scolding cheerfully, prevent
Arthur from running away, acknowledge the rights of the
complainers with gestures, take turns imitating the
complainers. For a while they have fun, but then they become
bored and leave.*)

Daffy: Quiet up there! You're all so loud that we can't play in
peace!!

All complainers (*to each other after a short pause of horror*):
That's—that's the limit! Did they say *we* were too loud?
Where's their manners? Those brats! Loud?! I'll show
them who's loud! Police! Police!

III

*In front of another house. The children run on stage out of
breath.*

Bizzy: Boy, it's getting worse and worse.

Dizzy: Where are we supposed to go if we want to play?

Bizzy: Hey, keep it down! Otherwise we'll get booted out of
here, too.

Dizzy (*quietly*): "This used to be a good neighborhood until
you kids moved in!"

Daffy: "Even the dogs bark with muzzles on!"

Arthur: "Only peace-loving citizens live here!". . .

Daffy: How would you know? You're new here.

Arthur: "For 100 years I've lived in this house! For 100 years and no one's ever dared to pee on the walls—" (*The others have to laugh. Arthur continues proudly.*) "For 100 years I've been sitting by my window gossipping, and if you don't leave me in peace—"

Bizzy: Yeah? Then what?

Arthur: "...then you'll get something you've never gotten before!

Daffy: Good! I've always wanted to get something I've never had before!

Arthur: "If I were your mother..."

Bizzy: Eeeeeks!

Arthur: "I'd show you how to behave!"

Dizzy: Oh, show us!

Arthur: Stand up straight when I talk to you! (*The others form a line. Arthur strides up and down. After every sentence one of the children overreacts and gets hit on the head by Arthur.*) Now, show me how a nice, well-brought up boy behaves! (*Daffy bows and belches. Arthur pretends to hit him on the ear.*) Bam!

Daffy: Ow!

Arthur: Now show me how a nice, well-brought up girl behaves. (*Dizzy curtsies and farts.*) Bam!

Dizzy: Ow!

Arthur: And you! You haven't combed your hair! (*Arthur hits air because Bizzy ducks.*)

Bizzy: Bam!

Arthur (*to Dizzy*): Show me your hands. (*Slaps them.*) I've told you a hundred times not to run around with dirty hands! (*Slaps.*) Bam!

Bizzy: Ow!

Arthur (*to Daffy, who spits in his hands and wipes them on his pants*: Show me your hands! Well! Almost clean! Other side! (*Daffy turns around.*) Not like that, dummy, your hands! Aha! Do you call those clean fingernails? (*Slaps hard.*)

Daffy: Ow! You're really hitting me!!

(*Bizzy, Dizzy, and Daffy charge Arthur upon a given signal.*)

Bizzy: You're mean!

Arthur: No, I'm not. I only seem mean. After all, I only want the best for you.

Dizzy: Not so loud, otherwise somebody'll start complaining!

Daffy: Hey, nobody's shouting at us!

Arthur: Why isn't anybody shouting?

Bizzy: Really, no one's complaining!

Arthur: Hey, what's the matter? Maybe all those old grouches are dead asleep?

All (*go up to the house*): Wake up!! Hey you grouches, wake up! Old hags, c'mon out! (*They do this a few times. Maybe together with the audience.*)

Arthur: C'mon, we'd better get going before someone comes and catches us.

Bizzy: Maybe they've complained themselves to death?

Dizzy: Yeah, I've never heard of a landlord or a super that didn't complain about noise.

Daffy: Hey, maybe the house is empty!

Dizzy: I think you're right. There aren't any curtains or shades on the windows.

Daffy: C'mon, let's look in the window. . . . (*Daffy lifts Bizzy onto his shoulders.*)

Bizzy: Can't see anything.

Arthur: Let me look.

Bizzy: You can't see any better!

Arthur: But I know how to get the window open. (*Takes out his knife.*) With this. (*He fiddles with the window frame.*)

Bizzy: Yeah, go on!

Dizzy: Quick, we'll make sure that no one comes!

Arthur (*opens the window*): Man, is it dirty here!

Daffy: You don't happen to have a light, do you?

Arthur: I always come prepared. Here! (*Pulls out a small flashlight.*)

Bizzy: Do you see anything?

Arthur: Just a lot of junk.

Daffy: Well, let's go inside then.

Arthur: Are you crazy? You want to break into a house?

Bizzy: What do you mean "break in"? The window's already open.

Arthur: Yeah, after I opened it.

Dizzy: It's fun to break in.

Arthur: But it's against the law.

Bizzy: Yeah, well, we just want to play, and they won't let us play on the streets. So we're going in!

Arthur: What if someone sees us?

Daffy: Who could see us if nobody lives here?

Bizzy: C'mon. Climb in!

Arthur: You could go to jail for this!

(*Bizzy laughs at him.*)

Daffy (*to Dizzy*): Well? What do you think?

Dizzy (*shrugs her shoulders at first and then asks the audience*): You think we should climb in there?

Audience: Yeeees!

Dizzy (*to Arthur*): You don't have to come if you don't want to...

Arthur: Me? You're not gonna leave me out of this! Of course I'm coming. You think I'm scared or something? (*Daffy helps Arthur climb through the window.*)

IV

The house from inside. Scene change to open stage using only flashlights. Arthur climbs through the window and begins to shine his flashlight inside. Bizzy pulls herself through the window after him.

Bizzy: Hey, help me! —Did you find anything yet?

Arthur: Over here—an old oven...

Bizzy: Great, then we won't have to freeze in winter...

Dizzy (*climbs through the window next*): Come here a second! We've got to help pull Daffy through. (*They do it with groans.*)

Daffy: Well, here we are. —How does it look?

Bizzy: Shhh!

Arthur: It's pretty dark in here...

Bizzy: Be quiet—I heard a noise!

Dizzy: Oh, it was probably just some ghost creeping around!

Arthur: What do you mean "ghost?"

Daffy: Booo!

Arthur (*scared*): Hey, cut that out! There are no such things as ghosts!

Daffy: Then why'd you jump?

Bizzy: It might have been a rat instead...I mean, one of those sweet, tiny...

Arthur: Eeeks! Ahhh! I think I just stepped on a rat!

Dizzy: Oww! That was my foot, stupid!

Arthur (*finds a bag of sugar cubes*): Hey, look here!

Bizzy: Oh good! Give me some!

Arthur: No, I found it! And now it belongs to me!

Bizzy: Nothing belongs to you!

Arthur: But I saw it first!

Dizzy: That doesn't mean that it automatically belongs to you. Whatever we find in this house belongs to all of us because we all climbed in together.

Arthur: What do you mean! Who was the one who climbed in first, huh? Me!

Daffy: *Someone* had to be first.

Dizzy: And you never would have made it without Daffy.

Bizzy: And you wouldn't have had the guts if we hadn't kept guard.

Arthur: But I found the bag by myself, so it belongs to me.

Bizzy: What's inside?

Arthur: Sugar cubes.

Bizzy: But you don't want to eat all of them by yourself.

Arthur: Of course not. I want to share them! But they belong to me no matter what.

Daffy: Well, if you're gonna share them anyway, then it doesn't matter who they belong to.

Arthur: Oh yes it does! I saw the bag first!

Dizzy: O.K. then! I sat on the oven first, so it belongs to me.

Daffy: And I was the first to say we should look in the window, so the window belongs to me.

Bizzy: And I was the first to look into the room, so the room belongs to me. Get away from there!

Arthur: Well—for all I care...(*Gives Daffy the bag.*) Here, pass them out...

Bizzy: Hope there's no rat poison in it...

(*Daffy becomes frightened and spits some sugar out.*)

Dizzy: Mmm, looks brand new to me. (*Sticks a cube in her mouth.*) Tastes like it, too.

Bizzy (*with sugar in her mouth*): I'm gonna check out the other rooms. —Anyone want to come with me?

Arthur: me.

(*Both leave.*)

Dizzy: Man, Daffy, such a big house, and just for us!

Daffy: We can make as much noise as we want here. (*He discovers an empty picture frame, holds it in front of his face and makes faces.*) Hey, look! A neat picture, huh?

Dizzy: Now that's what I call great art. What's the picture called?

Daffy: Guess.

Dizzy: "Grumble Puss."

Daffy: Noo! "Television announcer who has just been bitten by a monkey!" —And what's this? (*Scratches his ear.*)

Dizzy: A dog scratching himself.

Daffy: Right!

Dizzy: Now it's my turn. (*Behind the frame with mouth wide open.*) Njaah!

Daffy: One of those pukey opera singers.

Dizzy (*shakes her head*): Njaah!

Daffy: A fly eater...

Dizzy: A what?

Daffy: A fly eater. He waits until a fly flies into his mouth, and then he shuts his mouth and eats it.

Dizzy: Nooo, a woman at the dentist. (*Dizzy gives the picture frame back.*)

Daffy: And who's this? (*furious man looking out with his hand over his eyes.*)

Dizzy: I know, a teacher who's taking some kids on a trip, and he gets mad at them because they won't stay together.

Daffy: Nope.

(*Dizzy asks the children in the audience who make suggestions.*)

Daffy: No, it's the owner of a house who can't believe his eyes because four strange children are playing in his house.

Dizzy: You mean somebody might come and chase us out?

(*Daffy nods.*)

Dizzy: But we're not disturbing anyone!

Daffy: Oh yes we are! The landlord. Each house has an owner. Even when it's empty.

Dizzy: Boy, everything everywhere belongs to somebody. Everything! Right?

Daffy: "Get out of my house! That's mine! The forest and the fields are mine, too! And you're not allowed to walk there because that's my property! Everything here belongs to me! Because what's mine is mine!"

Yours or Mine

Dizzy: Hey, let me ride your bike?

Daffy: No! No! It's mine!

Dizzy: But you're not using it.

Daffy: I don't care, it's mine.

Dizzy: You said you won't need it today.
      Why can't I use it anyway?

Daffy: 'Cause what's mine is mine.
      Mine! Mine! Mine!

Dizzy: 'Cause what's his is his!
      (*sarcastically*) Fine! Fine! Fine!

Daffy: Yours or mine?
      That's all we ever hear!

Dizzy and Daffy: Yours or mine?
      We really shouldn't care!

Daffy: Why are we fighting over things?

Dizzy: Why don't we try to share things?
      Then we'd get, each one of us,

Daffy: Exactly what we need.

Dizzy: May I go in your house?
Daffy: No! No! It's mine!
Dizzy: But no one's living there!
Daffy: I don't care, it's mine!
Dizzy: I promise we won't mess about, so you won't have to
    kick us out.
Daffy: But what's mine is mine!
    Mine! Mine! Mine!
Dizzy: But what's his is his!
    (*sarcastically*) Fine! Fine! Fine!
Daffy: Yours or mine?
    That's all we ever hear.
Dizzy and Daffy: Yours or mine?
    We really shouldn't care!... (*Continue refrain.*)

Dizzy: Mind if I ride your bike?
Daffy: Go right ahead! Why not?
Dizzy: It's a beauty of a bike!
Daffy: Ride as long as you like!
Dizzy and Daffy: Wouldn't that be really great
    if we would share and love, not hate.
    Then we'd all get, each one of us,
    just what we need!
    Then we'd all get, each one of us,
    just what we need!

(*The police officers Knick and Knock enter and move toward the window.*)

Knick: Here's the house, Knock.
Knock: Ahh! And where's the door?
Dizzy: Damn it, the owner's outside!
Knick: Over there, but unfortunately it's locked, Knock.
Knock: Oh. Well, then how do you always get in?
Knick: Right here through this nice little window.
Knock: Man! You think that's right, to climb through a
    window. What if a cop sees you?
Knick: But, Knock, we are the cops!

Knock: Well, that's different isn't it?

Knick: Your damned right it is.

Knock: Anyway, it's our duty to check and make sure no tramp's hiding in there, isn't it?

Dizzy: What should we do?

Daffy: Hide, what else? (*They hide.*)

Knock (*listens*): Hey, did you hear some noise in there?

Knick: Noise? No. (*Knocks on the window.*) Hello! Is there a noise in there?

Knock: Well, then, alley-oop, man! What are you waiting for? —You go first! (*Helps Knick climb in. He looks around anxiously.*)

Knick (*pulls Knock through the window*): There! Nice cosy place here, huh? A little dusty here and there.

Knock: You mean filthy. So this is your little hideout.

Knick: I always drink my coffee here.

Knock: What do you mean? Is this some sort of a cafe?

Knick: No, I always bring it with me. (*Takes out a thermos from his coat pocket. He pours coffee into a cup and offers Knock some.*)

Knock: And what if somebody sees us here?

Knick: Oh, stop worrying... Isn't it much nicer to drink coffee here than in the station where the chief is always after us? ...Hmmm, I'm pretty sure I left my sugar lying around here somewhere...

Daffy: Oh-oh, it's his sugar!

Knock: Hey, didn't you hear an echo just then? I'm positive I heard the word sugar!

(*Daffy lets the bag drop next to Knick.*)

Knick: Sugar? Yes. Look, I found it. Must have fallen out of my pocket. Half gone already.

(*During this incident, Arthur and Bizzy appear, and Daffy and Dizzy anxiously wave them back.*)

Dizzy (*to Bizzy*): Are you crazy? Don't come over here!

Knock: Crazy?! Did you say crazy?

Knick: Not that I know! But maybe I did...Oh, yes....Man, how I'd like to have this entire place for myself! That'd be crazy!

Knock: Yeah, it'd be fantastic! One room for shooting, one for training, gymnastics and wrestling. Then one for tin soldiers, and there'd probably be room for my collection of shrunken heads. Did I ever show them to you?

Knick: And I'd have room for my parakeets, one for my turtles, one for my rabbit, and one for my grandmothers to play ping-pong in!

Knock: Still, I don't think we should've climbed in here. That's not wise.

Knick: But we did it, Knock, and remember you're part of the crime...

Knock: The what?! Yeah—but only for today! Because—uh—well. I'm gonna check out the joint. Case the place. (*Goes in the direction of Arthur and Bizzy, then stops.*) Hey, c'mon!

Knick: The only thing you'll find here is a couple of rats...

Knock: Did you say rats?! (*Bizzy giggles.*) Hey, what's so funny? (*Renewed giggling.*)

Knick (*confused*): Oh. I thought it was you who laughed— (*Noise from Arthur*). —Take cover! (*Has trouble drawing his gun from his holster.*)

Knock: O.K.! Whoever's there, c'mon out! Don't try and pull anything, otherwise there'll be trouble! (*Policemen listen. Running in the dark.*)

Knick: Forget it. Probably just some termites...

Knock: A whole regiment of termites, huh? (*Laughs under tension.*) Well, whatever it is, we got no time to find out. Our break's over, and we'd better be going.

Knick (*sighs with relief and puts his things together*): Yeah, you're right. We better be going. It's a shame to leave. This house is really great, don't you think?

Knock: Of course it's great. I've always dreamed of owning a place like this.

Knick (*while climbing out*): That's about all you can do: dream. People like us can't afford such places.

Knock: You got to have a bundle of money to own a place like this!

Knick: Yeah, it's really nice...and comfortable.

Knock: Comfortable? You mean it's too comfortable. C'mon now, we'd better get out of here.

(*Both exit. Knick's cap is left behind. While the children begin speaking, Arthur picks it up.*)

Daffy: They're gone. You can come in.

Bizzy: Man oh man, they almost caught us!

Dizzy: Climbing in here like that just to have coffee...

Bizzy: So it was his sugar.

Daffy: And now he's taken it with him.

Arthur (*puts on the cap and cries*): Hands up! It's the police!

Daffy: Arthur the cop, just look at that!

Bizzy: With a real cop's hat!

Daffy and Dizzy: And it's really real!

Bizzy: Where'd you get it?

Arthur: I just borrowed it for awhile.

Bizzy: Who from?

Arthur: It belongs to one of the cops who was just here.

Dizzy: You crazy?!

Arthur: What d'you mean? You jealous?

Daffy: That means the cops will be coming back here to get the cap.

(*The policemen appear outside.*)

Dizzy: Now what'll we do?

Bizzy: We'll just put the cap on the window sill.

Daffy: Watch out!

(*Knick appears in the window. The children don't have any more time to hide and wait pressed to the back wall. Arthur is furthest back with the cap on.*)

Knock (*still outside*): Hurry up! Hurry up! We're going to be late!

Knick (*pulls him in*): I'm trying, I'm trying...

Knock: There! Now where'd you leave the thing? Huh?

Knick: Well, I thought I left it here—it's got to be here!...My God, nobody will think I'm a policeman without my cap—

Knock: Man! It's getting late, and I'm getting fed up!

Knick: That's easy for you to say, but if the chief gets ahold of me like this, he'll fire me for sure!...(*Stands petrified. Sees the children and points at them.*) There!

Knock: Well, finally! Now let's clear out of here! (*Sees the children for the first time.*) Wha-what—oh, no—!! I think we caught our little rats!

Knick: You mean little termites. —

Bizzy: We're children!

Knock: Don't be smart!

Knick: Come over here!

Knock: Up against the wall. —Let's frisk them! (*They frisk the children.*)

Knick: What d'you think you're doing here?

Dizzy: Playing...

Knock: Playing! You're not playing. You've broken into a strange house. You're destroying private property!

Daffy: What d'you mean?

Knick (*points at Arthur*): My cap!!

Knock: And you're stealing from the police!!!! Give me the cap! (*Takes it and throws it to Knick who puts it on. He breathes a sigh of relief.*) Your names!

Daffy: Our names?

Knock (*pulls out a pad*): I'm sure your parents will be happy to learn all about this.

Dizzy: They want our names? (*Murmur, then*):

All: Well, nice knowing you. We've got to be going. it's getting late.

Knick: No you don't, wise guys! You're coming with us!

knock: Right down to the station! Go on!!! You first!

Arthur: Me first?

Knock: Hop to it! (*Leads them one by one to the window. The children try to get away a few times but don't succeed. Daffy and the others join in quietly, gritting their teeth*):

Just one is no one.
Two can get much more done
The grown-ups tell us what to do.
They still boss us around.
But soon we'll be more and more,
then watch us go to town!

V

Police station. Left, slanted on the side wall a long bench.
Right, a table and three chairs. In the middle, from the back
wall forward, the semblance of a partition. Knock is the first
through the door leading Arthur by the arm. The other
children follow, then Knick. The children are still singing the
song. Arthur is the only one who is very worried.

Knick: For the last time, keep it down, or...

Knock: Or, we'll let you have it but good!

Bizzy: We thought you'd like to be entertained.

Knock: Sit down! (*Goes with Knick to the table.*)

Daffy: Where?

Knick: On the bench over there.

Dizzy: All of us on one bench?

Knick: Oh, you'll manage it...

Knock: It's big enough for all your little asses!

Knick: Hey, Knock, watch your language in front of the kids!

Knock: What'd you want me to say to these brats: "Sit down
on your delicate rear ends?" (*The children examine the
bench for dust and test it to see if it is sturdy.*) Sit down, I
said! Or—

Daffy: or I'll call the police! (*The children laugh.*)

Knick: Man, this is going to be a bad day... Now, come on
and sit down, kiddies. Show your Uncle Knick how good
you can be!

Bizzy: O.K.. We're sitting... (*Knick at the typewriter.*)

Knock: Now, out with your names! The cap stealer first!
What's your name?

Arthur (*who is on the outside*): My—my name is Ar—

Bizzy: Ow! My ankle! I sprained my ankle! (*Dizzy has shoved
her off the bench in order to play along.*) Oww! (*Limps,
then falls down. Daffy and Dizzy stand up immediately
and go over to her.*)

Daffy and Dizzy: Oh, your poor ankle. Where does it hurt? We better carry her to the hospital!

Knock: Sit down!!

Knick (*examines her foot*): All right, cool it! You O.K.? Let me look at your foot. This little piggy went to market... (*He tickles her foot. She laughs.*)

Knock: That's no piggy, that's a ham. Now, get over there and sit down! (*Turning to Arthur*): I asked you what your name is!

Arthur: My—

Daffy: Daffy!

Knick: What do you mean Daffy?

Daffy: My name is Daffy.

Knock: I don't want to know what *your* name is!

Bizzy (*who is now sitting next to Arthur*): Bizzy!

Knock: I don't mean you, I mean—

Dizzy: Excuse me, my name's Dizzy.

Knock (*in quiet desperation before bursting*): Look, I've had it! I'm gonna count to three, and if you don't give me your real names, I'll—I'll

Bizzy, Dizzy, Daffy: Bizzy, Dizzy, Daffy!

Knock: Tell me now, do I look like a dumb cop?

Knick: No, no, you look perfectly smart to me.

Knock (*to Arthur*): Stand up! (*Arthur springs to attention. After a split second, the others do likewise.*)

Knock: Sit down!!! —You there! Step forward! (*All four step forward.*) Sit down!!! —That boy there! Stand up! (*Arthur and Daffy stand up. Knock jumps furiously at the children, pulls Arthur away, and holds him by the collar.*) So, my boy, now we'll get down to business! Name?!

Arthur: A-a-ar-

Bizzy: I've got to go! I can't hold it in any longer!

Daffy: I've got to go worse than you!

Knick: Well, if you gotta go, you gotta go.

Knock: What kind of a monkey circus is this anyway!

Daffy: Monkey circus? I thought this was the police station! We must be in the wrong place...

Bizzy: Oh-oh, I can't hold it in any longer!

Dizzy: Me, too!

Knick: Now cut this crap out! What do you take us for?

Arthur: M-m-may I go to the bathroom, too?

Knock: Totally out of the question!! First answer me!

Knick (to Daffy, who is opening his fly): Hey, what do you think you're doing!

Daffy: If I'm not allowed to leave the room, then I'll just have to pee on the wall...

(Arthur also begins to fumble with his pants.)

Bizzy: Man! I can't hold it in either!

Knock: Christ! Go ahead!! All of you! But make it snappy!! Second door on the left!

(Children exit.)

Knick: This is going to be a bad day for us. I can feel it in my bones.

Knock: Maybe. But not for us, Knick! You don't think I'm gonna let myself be made a fool of by these midgets, do you?!

Knick: Maybe they haven't done anything wrong?

Knock: Let's wait and see. We've got to take them one at a time! We'll get nothing out of them if we take them together!

Knick: That's for sure. The best thing is to keep them separate. —Still, I feel it in my bones: It's gonna be a bad day...

Order Makes up Half Your Life

Knick and Knock: Oh the evil times are coming!
　　　You can see the problems mounting.
　　　There's no respect at all, no more.
　　　The kids now act like outlaws!
　　　So we need law and order to keep
　　　our country clean!
　　　And who's the most important then?
　　　It's us, of course, the law men!

Refrain: For order makes up half your life.
　　　Without order

the entire earth would crumble.
Keep order
and order will keep you.
Without order,
order would become disorder.
Only those who love order and
cleanliness
will get very far,
and it's only those
who love order and
cleanliness
who'll be a real success.

Knick and Knock: Oh the boys and girls today
don't know or want to obey.
They're always asking questions,
and we don't have good suggestions.
They don't have manners or respect.
The whole world's going to the dogs.
And who's supposed to check this then?!
It's us, of course, the law men!

Refrain: For, order makes up half your life.
Without order
the entire earth would crumble.....

Knock: O.K. Go out and bring in the boy who had your cap
on. (*Knick leaves.*) Wait till you see how I break him
down and make him talk. (*Calls after Knick*): And lock
the other three in the waiting room! (*While Knick is
outside, Knock practices his technique of making stern
and menacing gestures for the inquiry. From outside
come loud cries of protest.*)

Knick: Cut it out! I'm just carrying out my orders!

(*Leads Arthur in. Knock in the meantime has tactically moved
a chair for Arthur in the center of the room.*)

Arthur: But why me?

Knick: I don't know why. I'm just doing my duty.

Knock: So, my boy. Sit down! —And now, if you're smart, you'll tell us everything! Don't think you can make monkeys out of us.

Knick: He who laughs best laughs last!

Knock: Thank you. —Now: Which one of you is the ring leader?

Arthur: Ring—what's that?

Knock: *I'm the one* who asks the questions! You answer!

Arthur: But I really don't know what a ring leader is—

Knick: Listen, kid, you know damned well what a leader is.

Arthur: It wasn't me! Besides, we don't even have a leader. We climbed into the house all by ourselves.

Knick: Which one of you four is the leader?

Arthur: No one. —All of us together...

Knock: Yeah, well, who was the first to get the idea?

Arthur: What idea?

Knock: What idea?! To climb into the house, naturally. Well! Was it your idea?

Arthur: No!

Knock: Whose was it then?

Arthur: It wasn't mine—and I really don't know whose it was.

Knick: But one person always takes charge and tells everyone what to do—

Arthur: I just met them all today—!

Knock: Oh, come off it, will you!

Knick: And even if you did, you've gotten yourself in with fine company! Real criminals! Now listen to me, boy, tell us who came up with the idea to climb into the house, and everything will be all right. —Otherwise, remember the old saying: caught together, hung together!

Arthur: I'm telling the truth. I really don't know anything...

Knock: Now it's my turn. —Do you know what happens to children who tell lies and take the wrong path? They're put in detention homes! And when you're older, in reformatories! And then in prison! You don't want to go to prison, do you?

Arthur: No! I never want to go to prison!

Knick: Don't worry. You won't go to prison...You're much

too young.

Knock (to Knick): Quiet, it's my turn now. (*To Arthur*): Sit up straight when I'm talking to you! —If you don't open your mouth pretty soon, I'm gonna give you what they call a knuckle sandwich!

Knick: Take it easy, Knock. He's only a kid!

Knock: Kid or no kid, he'd better answer! Tell me the truth now, or we'll go to your teacher and your parents and tell them what a lousy little criminal you've turned into!

Arthur: Please don't go to my parents! I'll tell you everything you want to know!

Knock (breathes a sigh of relief. He has a feeling of triumph and takes it easy): Well, my friend, now we understand each other. Knick, take all this down. O.K. First, your name.

Arthur: Are you going to tell my parents?

Knock: Damn right we are!

Arthur: Then I won't tell you my name.

(*Knick must laugh a little because Knock's tactics have obviously backfired. Knock looks at him furiously.*)

Knock: Just tell us which one of you was the instigator!

Arthur: What's an instigator?

Knick: The one who starts everything.

Knock: Look, that's all we want to know.

Arthur (who is aware that Knock is now giving in a little): I'm no stool pigeon.

Knick: Now that's a real dumb word. All we want you to do is to help us out.

Arthur: By being a stool pigeon.

Knock: You better start talking quick, or we'll make sure you wind up in reform school!

Arthur: If that's the case, then—Bizzy.

Knock: Aha. Bizzy. Write that down, Knick.

Arthur: Or Dizzy.

Knock: Or Dizzy. Very interesting. Have you got it, Knick?

Arthur: Or Daffy.

Knock: Or Daffy. —Or Daffy? Bizzy or Dizzy or Daffy? All three of them again! (*Threatening him.*) Now I've had enough, you little—

Knick: Keep your cool, Knock!

Arthur: If you don't believe me, ask Daffy.

Knock: So, it was Daffy.

Arthur: No, I just mean that he would know before I would—I don't know anything because I'm new, but if you get Daffy, two heads are certainly better than one—

Knock: Yes, yes. Two heads. So that you can play your tricks together again. Well, I'm fed up with your tricks!

Knick: You mean: four eyes see more than two.

Arthur (*thankfully*): Yes.

Knick: You see!

Knock (*resignedly*): Be my guest—bring them in—you'll soon see what you'll get from them.

Knick: Hindsight's better than foresight.

Knock: Will you spare me your stupid sayings!! (*Knick leaves. Knock and Arthur avoid each other's glances. Outside, tumult.*)

The girls: Help! It's not fair! What are you doing to them!

Knick (*comes in with Daffy*): Sit down next to your—uh, friend there. (*Daffy sits down.*) There. —(*Looks at Knock.*)

Knock: Go ahead. I've lost my desire.

Knick: Only the strong will inherit the earth. —Now Daffy, which one of you—now listen carefully—which one of you was the first to have the idea to climb into the house?

Daffy: I won't tell.

Knick: That's not polite.

Knock: You're gonna stay here in the police station until you open your big fat trap, understand?

Daffy: O.K. I'll talk.

Knick: Go ahead. I'm listening.

Daffy: But not now.

Knick: What do you mean, not now? When then?

Daffy: When the girls are let in here!

Knock: Why do they have to be here? You can talk just as well alone.

Daffy: Of course I can. But we were all together in the house, so we'll only talk about it when we're all together!

Knick: Together...together....Oh, go on and bring them in!

Knock: Why me?

Knick: Why me, am I your servant? I did it the last time. Go on, the boys want to talk. Go on!

Daffy: Yeah, get a move on!

Knock: O.K. But you take the responsibility!! (*Leaves.*)

Knick: I'm not afraid of responsibility.

Daffy: Don't let him get you upset...

Knick: But maybe he'll squeal to the chief.

Daffy: So, what have you done? Nothing.

Knock (*pushes the girls in*): There! On the bench! (*The children greet each other with loud hellos. The boys also sit down on the bench.*)

Knock: Get off of there! Get away from each other! (*Pushes the boys off their places.*) Quiet!! (*The boys go back to the bench.*)

Daffy (*and then the other children*): Quiet!! Didn't you hear me? Quiet! Quiet! You'd better be quiet! I'm losing my patience! Etc.

Knock: Quiet!!!

Bizzy: That's what I've been saying the whole time!

Knock (*to Knick*): Now we'll see whether they keep their promise.

Daffy: What kind of promise?

Knick: Ah—why you just promised to tell us everything if we brought the girls in!

Bizzy: Is that so?

Daffy: Noo, we didn't promise that.

Knock: What?!

Daffy: We only promised that we would tell *something* but not everything.

Knock: Then you lied to us!

Knick: No—actually it was more a trick.

Knock: A lie!

Knick: A trick!! (*They banter back and forth awhile.*)

Knock: Have you been drinking, Knick? Doing the same

things these here brats do, jumping on my back like a—a

Knick: I'm only trying to find out the truth. The truth must always prevail in the end.

Knock: And whoever's dumb stays dumb. There's no cure for that!

Knick: Right! That's why I forgot my cap in the house, otherwise none of this would have happened! If I'd put it on—isn't it much better to have a cap in the hand than a bird on the head??

Knock: I can't stand your dumb sayings anymore!

Knick: And I can't stand your yelling anymore because whoever yells into the woods—

Knock: I'm not yelling!!!!! I'm completely calm, completely calm. Absolutely calm.

Knick: O.K. then we can proceed quietly. Now, which one of you was the first to have the idea of climbing into the house?

Daffy: All of us together.

Knick: All of you together?

All: All of us, all of us together.

Knock: No one asked you!

Knick: And no one asked you. So, do me a favor, Knock, keep out of this! It's my case now. —Let's put it this way: *why* did you actually break into the house?

Arthur: Break into...?

Knock: Yes, break into!

Daffy: We were just playing in there. Certainly there's no law against playing...

Knick: You're not allowed to do that.

Dizzy: What? Not play?

Knick: Not play!

Bizzy: But we're allowed to break in!

Knick: Right, you're allowed to—now cut that out!

Knock: Don't let them lead you around by the nose, Knick!

Daffy (*to Arthur*): Lead him around by the nose! Should I lead you around by the nose? (*Grabs him by the nose and leads him around.*)

Arthur: And now I'll lead you! (*The girls do the same.*)

Knick: Enough of this! Now sit down! —Why did you climb
    into the house?

Daffy: We just wanted to play!

Knick: Playing on private property is forbidden!

Daffy: Where else can we play?

Knock: What about a playground?!

Daffy: He wants to give us a playground! Oh, boy!

Knock: Now stop that! I meant, you should go to one!

Daffy: But there aren't any around here.

Knick: Then—why don't you play at home!

Dizzy: We're not allowed to.

Daffy: If I do this just once—(*He honks.*)—then four
    neighbors start complaining—

Knock: Quie-e-et! You brat!

Daffy: That's exactly what they say! How'd you know that?

Knick: Then you could play in the yard or in one of the courts
    of the buildings.

Bizzy: That's forbidden.

Knick: Or in the street?

Arthur: Too dangerous. Besides, the cars take up too much
    space.

Knick: Uh-uh—I'm running out of suggestions. . . .

Daffy: Why aren't there any playgrounds around here?

Knock: Because playgrounds are too expensive, you idiot!

Arthur: What would a playground cost? As much as a car?

Knick: More. Certainly more!

Daffy: As much as a tank?

Knick: No, not that much. For a tank you could build at least
    20 playgrounds.

Bizzy: Ooooh! Then why doesn't anyone do it?

Knick (*to Knock*): Yeah, why doesn't anyone do it?

Knock: Because a tank is more important than 20
    playgrounds! —Don't ask me, ask the children out there!!

Daffy (*asks the audience*): Do you think a tank is more
    important than a playground?

Knick: I think a tank's more important than a playground. At
    least, I'm pretty sure. Not positive. Anyway, you really
    should have a place to play where you won't disturb

anyone.

Dizzy: That's just what we were doing!

Bizzy: We weren't disturbing anyone when we were in that house.

Arthur: Except maybe you, while you were drinking your coffee...

Knick: Maybe we should just send these kids home with a warning?

Knock: That's out of the question! These wise guys aren't gonna get away with breaking into private houses and stealing things from the police. Their parents got to know about this so they can punish them.

Knick: Punish them, yes—spare the rod and spoil the child!

Knock (*to the boys*): Now, which one of you two was the instigator?

Arthur: Not me!

Knock (*to Daffy*): Then it was you! —You! —You! --You!

Daffy: You!

Knock: I've never met such stubborn brats in my whole life! (*To Knick*): I'm gonna have a try with the girls. —Well, you two, so you're Bizzy and Dizzy.

Bizzy: Yes, we already know that.

Dizzy: Are you cold?

Knock: No, why?

Dizzy: Because you keep rubbing your hands together like that....

Knock: Now don't try to get me off the track! I want you to answer my questions, you hear! —Now, you do understand, girls, don't you? You don't want to get Uncle Knock mad, do you?

Bizzy: Do you have a toothache?

Knock: What do you mean toothache?

Bizzy: Because you keep making such funny faces!

(*Knick coughs.*)

Knock (*controls himself with effort*): Now—that's enough fooling around. Please, just tell me which one of the boys had the—uh, nice idea to climb into the house. Huh? (*He winks at them.*)

Dizzy: Oh, you have something in your eye?

Knock: Noooooo!

Knick (*composed*): Now we know that you two actually had nothing whatsoever to do with the whole thing—

Dizzy and Bizzy: Oh yeah! Why not?

Knick: I mean, the boys gave you the idea, of course.

Bizzy: What do you mean, gave us the idea?

Knock: Well, nice little girls like yourselves—ahem—would never get the idea of breaking into a house—

Bizzy: And why not?

Dizzy: Why couldn't it have been us who gave the idea to the boys?

Knick and Knock: No! No! Not you two! That's impossible!

Knock: Boys are more devilish than girls—filled with more energy.

Knick: Shrewder! More daring!

Knock: They're always the leaders! Stronger, smarter—definitely superior!

Bizzy: Stronger?

Dizzy: Shrewder?

Bizzy: Smarter?

Dizzy: And all girls are dumb, huh?

Whoever Says Girls Are Dumb

Both: Whoever says girls are dumb,
whoever says girls just act silly,
whoever says girls are shy
has got no brains! No brains!
Whoever says girls are scaredy cats,
whoever says they're cry babies
and always grumble and complain,
has got no brains, no brains at all!

Girls are just as sly as boys.
Girls are just as fresh—and quick and smart.
Girls are just as brave and strong as boys.
And they can also take a lot.

Whoever says girls are weak,
whoever says girls just act goofy,
whoever says that girls are zany,
has got no brains! No brains!
Whoever says girls are sissies,
are tattletales and troublesome
and make mistakes because they're dumb,
has got no brains, no brains at all!

Girls are just as sly as boys.
Girls are just as fresh — and quick and smart.
Girls are just as brave and strong as boys.
And they can also take a lot.

Knock: Now I've had enough! You think that just because
there are four of you, you can get away with anything!
(*Bizzy begins to cough.*)
Knick: Does she have a cold?
Bizzy: No!
Knock: She doesn't have anything contagious, does she?
Daffy: You never know. (*Coughs too, bumps Bizzy. She
coughs with a gasp.*)
Knick: Sounds like whooping-cough.
Dizzy: She caught it from me! (*Coughs too, goes toward
Knock.*)
Knock: So it is contagious! At least, cough in another
direction!
Bizzy: I have to go home to take my cough medicine!
Dizzy: Can we all go now?
Knock: No! You still don't seem to understand what the game
here is!
Bizzy: Well, if it is a game, it's a pretty shitty one!
Knock: Watch your language!! You've broken into a private
house, and that's trespassing! — According to criminal law
123, trespassing can be punished with up to three months
in prison!
Dizzy: Then you're sitting in the same boat!
Knock: What do you mean?

Dizzy: Because you broke into a private house, too! That's what we call—

Arthur: trespassing!

Daffy: Yeah, we saw you!

Bizzy: According to criminal law 123, you can get up to three months in prison! —You said so yourself.

Knock: Now listen here! Don't you go mixing things up! What we did is something entirely different. As policemen we have the duty to—

Dizzy: to drink coffee in strange people's houses!

Bizzy: Don't forget, we saw you!

Daffy: All four of us. Arthur, too! Right?

Knock: Now that's enough! (*Loses his temper.*) I'm gonna start swinging pretty soon!

Knick: Knock, control yourself!

Knock: Me control myself! What about them, big mouth!

Knick: Look, maybe it'd be better if we just sent the children home with a warning after all?

Daffy: Can we go now?

Knock: Well—as far as I'm concerned. (*The children jump up.*) Only after you give me your names!

Bizzy: Always the same garbage. . .

Knick: Maybe just one of them is enough.

Knock: Oh, all right. The cap stealer stays here!

Arthur: No, I won't!

Children: Right on, Arthur!

Knock: You other kids, get out of here! Scram! Beat it, quick!

Daffy: No, we're not going without Arthur.

Arthur: No, we're not going without me.

Knock: We'll see about that. (*Starts for the children. At a horn signal, the children link arms and sit on the floor. Knock tries furiously to pull them up. Knick tries, too. He talks to them in a friendly way, but the children scream loudly.*)

Knick: Hey, Knock, cool it! That's going too far! (*Tries to tear Knock from the children.*)

Knock: Get your hands off me!

Knick: They're only kids!

Knock: Tell me, whose side you on anyway?

Knick: I'm for justice.

Knock: Then you're for the cops.

Knick: I'm for the cops when the cops stand for justice.

Knock: Do you know what you are! A fink! A finky traitor!

Knick: Now you've picked the straw that broke the camel's back! One more word, and, and—

Knock: And—and what?

Knick: You've treated these children—like—like a gorilla! And I'm gonna report you!

Knock: You're gonna report me? You don't have a single thing to report! If anyone has anything to report, it's me! For not carrying out my orders.

Knick: You don't have any right to give me orders!

Knock: We'll see about that!

Knick: Damned right! We'll see about that!

Knock: I'm gonna take this case to the chief!

Knick: You do that! Just go ahead and do that!

Knock: Good! I'm gonna do that!

Knick: Well, go on. What are you waiting for?

Knock: I—I don't want anything more to do with this whole business!! (*Exits. The children rejoice.*)

Knick: I knew it. I could feel it in my bones. A bad day! A bad, bad day!

Bizzy: A good day!

Daffy: You were fantastic!

Knick: Well, time to leave, kids! Go, go! Get out of here! Go play!

Children: Where? Where are we supposed to play?

Knick: Don't start that again. And don't ask me. I have no idea!

(*Children ask the audience where they should play until they come upon the answer: simply to stay at the station and play there.*)

Arthur: Of course!

Bizzy: Good idea!

Dizzy: If we can't play anywhere else, then we can stay here and play!

Daffy: It's almost as nice here as it was in that great huge house! Come on. What should we play?

Arthur: In a police station? Cops and robbers of course! I'll play the—nooo...(*To Knick*): Do you want to play the Chief?

Knick (*embarrassed*): Me—the Chief—that would be something!

Dizzy: We're the robbers!

Bizzy: You have to catch us! (*Begin to race around the place.*)

Knick: Stop! Help! —Listen, as much as I'd like to be Chief— if you kids play here, I'll lose my job and then I won't be able to buy my children anything to eat. We'll have to think of another place to play in...

Dizzy: I only know of one other place.

Knick: Yes?!

Dizzy: The empty house.

Knick: NO!!

Daffy: Why not? We've already got four kids if we include Arthur here—

Arthur: Hey—I don't like the name Arthur anymore. I think it sounds stupid.

Bizzy: What do you mean? Arthur's a really neat name! Bizzy, Dizzy, Daffy, and Arthur—sounds great!

Arthur (*relieved*): If you think so—

Daffy: Listen. With Arthur we've got four, and if that's not enough, we'll invite all the children in the neighborhood to play with us. Then nobody'll be able to drive us out!

Knick: It'll never work. Then more cops will come, and more and more cops!

Dizzy: And more children—

Knick: And more cops—

Arthur: And the children will win because there's more of us!

Knick: Don't forget that the house *belongs* to—uh-uh—

Bizzy: Yeah—who does the house belong to anyway?

Knick: The house belongs to the city. It was bought to be rebuilt.

Daffy: And when will that happen?

Knick: Oh, that'll take some time...

Arthur: Then we can play inside until then!!

Knick: But that's too dangerous! What if a rafter should fall on one of your heads?

Bizzy: Can't the rafters be repaired?

Knick: Of course, but that costs money. At least 300 dollars.

Dizzy: 300 dollars isn't that much to pay—for a whole play house...

Arthur: That's the least they could do if they won't build a playground for us.

Knick: Well, first you have to put in a request—and that must be approved and then the approval has to be approved and signed and counter-signed. It's a whole bureaucratic process. A lot of red-tape.

Daffy: Couldn't you do that for us?

Knick: Yes— I suppose I could. (*Begins to type on the typewriter.*)

Arthur: And at the same time you can take down what should go inside the play house.

Bizzy: A slide on all the stairs!

Knick: Slide.

Daffy: And small drums and big drums and lots of horns.

Knick: Music chest.

Dizzy: And hammers and saws and pliers.

Knick: Tool chest.

Arthur: And lots of old clothes to dress up in!

Knick: Costume chest.

(*Children now ask the audience what they would like to have in the play house and dictate the answers to Knick.*)

Knick: Now, if it only works....

Daffy: It's got to work! Otherwise we'll get so many children together...

Arthur: and make so much noise, that they'll give us the house for sure!!

All: For sure!!

They now break into the refrain:

> Just one is no one.
> Two can get much more done.

The grown-ups tell us what to do.
They still boss us around.
But soon we'll be more and more,
then watch us go to town!

(*Knick keeps time by tapping rhythmically on the typewriter. They eventually march off stage toward the play house singing the song.*)

APPENDIX
Bizzy, Dizzy, Daffy and Arthur

For the Milwaukee production of this play, we decided to add two characters, the landlord and the police chief, in order to make the "enemy" of the children more identifiable. In the original play there is a tendency to focus too much on the police as the prime targets of the children's frustration. Since we saw the play as an attack on private property relations and authoritarianism, we shifted the focus to the landlord in an attempt to demonstrate the mediating role of the police who are generally used to legitimize exploitation. Here two alternatives are shown in Knick and Knock while the landlord represents the prevailing force of private property. In *showing* how the landlord manipulates the chief and the police, the power relations of society are clarified, and the children's struggle becomes concretized.

There are three scenes involving the landlord, and one with the chief. The same actor played the landlord and the chief in our production. The first scene with the landlord precedes the prologue. The next scene with the landlord comes immediately after scene three. The only scene with the chief takes place at the beginning of scene five right after Knock says: "Now, out with your names! The cap stealer first! What's your name?" The final scene with the landlord follows Knick's statement at the end of the play: "Now, if it only works."

* * * * *

Landlord Scene 1
Landlord stomps onto the stage. The audience is still moving around and is unprepared for his entrance. He appears to be hunting for someone. Finally, the landlord blows his top.
Landlord: Will you quiet down! C'mon. Quiet down out there! What do you think this is, a theater or something?!...
    (*Paces.*) I can't stand noise. And the tenants around here

can't stand noise either, and if there's any more peeps out
there, I'm gonna call the police. Understand?...
Anyway, you're not the troublemakers here. The real
troublemakers are sneaking around out there. Have you
seen them? I think there are three of them. I'm not sure.
But if I get my hands on them, I'll break their necks!...
Quiet out there! It's not funny. Are you sure you haven't
seen them?... You're no help to me!... I better go see if
my friend the chief of police can help. After all, I give
plenty of money to the patrolman's association and I pay
my taxes, so the Chief better help me. Maybe you kids
don't know, but he knows that money speaks!... I'll be
back. You wait and see! (*Exits.*)

*The garbage can has been standing in the middle of the
stage. Bizzy is in it. After the landlord exits, she pushes the top
off and jumps out. Then she blows her whistle and begins to
look for Dizzy and Daffy.*

* * * * *

Landlord Scene 2

*Landlord comes on stage. Dressed in a suit and overcoat. Hat.
Smokes a cigar which he puffs on vigorously. He paces up and
down the street as if looking for someone. Finally he turns to
the audience.*

Landlord: Hey, have you seen two cops around here?... One
    of them is huge (*jumps up to show how large*) and the
    other's a squirt. They're both dumb, but I need them.
    You see, I own some buildings on this block, and there's
    this gang of kids who are always making noise. I can't
    stand kids, can you? Animals are even worse, although
    sometimes it's a toss-up between kids and animals...
    Anyway, my poor tenants are always complaining, and I
    need the cops to chase these lousy kids off the block. It's
    either the kids or my tenants, and since I get rent from my
    tenants, I'm gonna make sure those kids stay out of my
    territory.

(*Knick and Knock appear on the scene.*)

Landlord: There you are! Hey, c'mon over here.

Knock: You Mr. Crock?

Landlord: Who do you think I am, Mr. Jock?

Knock: I'm Knock.

Landlord: My name's Crock not Knock.

Knock: But I said Knock.

Crock: I know you said Knock, but the name's Crock.

Knock: No, it's not, it's Knock.

Landlord: And I said Crock, you fink!

Knick: Now, calm down you guys. I'll settle it. You said Crock and he said Knock.

Landlord: I don't care if he said Knock.

Knick: You don't understand.

Landlord: Sure, I understand. You guys have either been drinking, or you're trying to put something over on me. My name's Crock, and it's gonna stay Crock.

Knock: And my name's Knock, and it's gonna stay Knock.

Knick: Now do you get it?

Landlord: Sure, I get it, and I bet your name is Shock!

Knick: No, it's Knick.

Landlord: Ho, ho, Knick and Knock. What a pair of names! Knick-Knock, Knock-Knick. It's like snap, crackle and pop. Ho, ho!

Knock: You're not doing too bad yourself with a name like Crock.

Knock: I can think of a lot of things that can rhyme with Crock.

Landlord: Now, cut that out!

Knick: All right, all right. Now what did you ask us to come over here for?

Landlord: I didn't ask you. I *told* your chief to send somebody here right away! Maybe you two don't know who I am?

Knock: Sure I do. You're Crock and I'm Knock.

Landlord: Cut that out! It just so happens that I own half this block, Knock, and I want some respect!

Knock: Is that why you asked us to come here?

Landlord: Of course not!

Knick: Well, why then?

Landlord: It's quite simple, and I hope that you numbskulls can get it through your thick heads: there's a band of hoodlums terrorizing the tenants on this street, and I want you to find them.

Knick: You mean real hoodlums. Tough guys with guns!?

Landlord: No, not really. They're about nine or ten or eleven.

Knick: You mean squirts like the kids out there. (*Points to the audience.*)

Knock: And the people here can't take care of them?

Landlord: Look, you're not supposed to ask the questions. Just do as you're told, or I'll tell the Chief! These kids make noise and disturb the entire neighborhood.

Knick: Why do they do that?

Landlord: How should I know? Probably because they play in the streets.

Knick: Children shouldn't play in the streets!

Knock: Where should they play?

Landlord: I don't give a damn where they play. All I know is that I don't want them playing around here. It's my property, and you're policemen, and I want you to do your duty. Is that clear?

Knick: Yeah, I guess so.

Landlord: You better know so, brother. I've got special connections to your Chief, and if you know what's good for you!

Knock: Well, now it's as clear as can be.

Landlord: Good! Now that we've settled that, I can stop wasting my time here. I've got some important business deals to make. (*Stamps off with a huff.*)

Knick: What a creep!

Knock: He's worse than my own landlord, and he's pretty bad.

Knick: I wouldn't want to be his tenant. Never in a million years!

Knock: Do you suppose we have to look for those kids?

Knick: If we don't, Crock will tell the Chief, and then we'll be in for trouble.

Knock: I guess we really should. I mean, if these kids are terrorizing the neighborhood.

Knick: It's our duty, Knock. We can look for awhile, and if we don't find them, I'll show you my hideout where we can drink some coffee.

Knock: Your hideout! Wow! Well, let's hope that we don't find them then.

Knick: Knock, how many times do I have to tell you, we're the police, and duty comes before pleasure.

Knock (as they leave): Please don't start in with your stupid sayings. . . .

* * * * *

Chief Scene

Knock: Now, out with your names! The cap stealer first! What's your name?

Arthur: My name is. . .

Chief (enters): Hey, what's all the commotion going on here?! What's up!

Knick: We caught them, chief!

Chief: Caught who!

Knock: The gang that was terrorizing Crock's street.

Chief: Yeah, well I don't want them terrorizing this precinct, you hear!

Knock: Sure, chief!

Chief: I want you to make fast work of these monkeys, hear!

Knick: Sure, chief!

Chief (turning to the children): As for you, you're gonna get a lesson that you'll never forget!

Daffy: Sure, chief.

Chief: What was that?

Dizzy: He said, sure, chief.

Chief: Cut that out. I don't like to be mimicked!

Bizzy: But he was only saying what Officers Knick and Knock said.

Chief: I don't care what Knick and Knock said! If you kids don't watch your step, you're gonna wind up in reform school!

(Arthur tries to keep the others quiet.)

Chief: I mean what I say, and if you don't believe me, you can ask these two gentlemen over here.

Knock: He means what he says.

Chief: Right! (*Turns to Knick and Knock.*) And if you two don't do a job on these kids, you'll hear from me. I don't want old Crock on my back complaining about his goddam property. So clear this up. (*Starts to leave.*)

Knick and Knock: Sure, chief!

Chief (*stands still in his tracks, turns*): Now, cut that out! (*Exits.*)

Knock: All right, kiddies. You heard what the chief said!

Knick: No more fooling around. Time's money!

Knock: Damn right, time's money, and besides we don't want the chief on our back. So I want your names and I want them fast. (*Swirls at Arthur.*) Out with it!

Arthur: Out with what?

Knock: Your name!

Arthur: My name's Ar—

* * * * *

Landlord Scene 3

Knick: Now, if it only works...

Daffy: It's just gotta work...

Landlord (*comes running in*): Hey, what's going on here? The chief just called me and told me that you caught the brats who were terrorizing my block, and now you sit there calmly talking to them! I want them thrown behind bars!

Knick (*standing*): Now calm down, Crock.

Bizzy: Who're you?

Crock: None of your business.

Arthur: That's my line.

Crock: I don't care whose line that is, it's none of your damned business!

Daffy: Hey, watch your language.

Crock: You watch your manners! Show some respect!

Dizzy: Who should we respect?

Crock: Your elders!

Daffy: Why should we respect our elders if they don't respect us?

Knick: Right, you've got to earn respect. Only the just will inherit the earth.

Crock: Will you stop all this double talk! I want these kids put behind bars. And I mean now!

Arthur: Who made you boss?

Crock: You keep this up and I'll...I'll

Bizzy: You'll call the police!

Crock: Right! I mean, wrong! Don't put words in my mouth.

Dizzy: You mean you don't want the police?

Crock: Of course I want the police!

Knick: I am the police. What do you want?

Crock: I want these brats arrested.

Knick: What for?

Crock: For terrorizing my block, for trespassing, for showing no respect to me...

Knick: As far as I can see, you're the one who seems to be terrorizing these kids.

Dizzy: Right on, Officer Knick.

Knick: And you're the one who chases the children off the streets and charges high rents and won't let people run their own lives!

Crock: Who do you think you are!

Knick: I'm the police, and I'm doing my duty, and if you don't get out of here before I count to ten, I'm going to arrest you for trespassing on public property!

Crock: You're nuts! You're supposed to protect the people from criminals.

Knick: That's just what I'm doing. In my book you are a criminal!

Crock: But, but...

Knick: No buts, get out of here, and make it quick!

Crock (*afraid*): You're no fair! I've got connections and money, so you better watch out! You better be nice to me!

Knick: I don't care about your connections and money! Get out before I arrest you for trying to bribe me!

Crock: I'll get even with you! Just wait and see! (*Runs off stage.*)

Bizzy: Crybaby!

Bizzy, Dizzy, Daffy, Arthur: You were fantastic! Great! Right on! Far out!

Knick: Thanks, thanks, kids, but we can't stop here.

Dizzy: What do you mean?

Knick: Well, old Crock is going to try to get even with us, so we've got to do something.

Arthur: Yeah, let's burn his houses down!

Daffy: Hey, that's stupid. We don't want anyone to get killed.

Arthur: You're right. I sort of lost my head. I mean, I got carried away.

Bizzy: That's OK, Arthur. We know you really meant well this time.

Dizzy: That still doesn't help us. We've got to think of something.

Knick: Look, Crock is just one big fat landlord, and just because he's rich doesn't mean that he can boss us around, especially when there are a lot of us.

Daffy: You better believe it!

Arthur: Yeah, if we get our friends to help...

Dizzy: And if we get our parents to help...

Bizzy: And if we march to city hall and show them how things really are...

Daffy: Then we can get what we want!

Knick: And I'll try to get my friends on the police force to help.

Bizzy: Gee, Knick, you're not so bad after all. In fact, you're fantastic!

Arthur, Dizzy, Daffy: Right!

Knick: Hey, I'm only doing my duty, guys. Nothing more. Just remember the old saying...

Bizzy, Dizzy, Daffy and *Arthur*: Oh, no! There he goes again!!

Knick: Wait a second! Give me a chance. The old saying is a new saying and it goes like this: just one is no one, two can get more done!

They all break into the song, and while singing it, they

encourage the audience to participate. The song ends abruptly
on "Then watch us go to town!"
Dizzy: Well, let's go to our new house.
Arthur: Yeah, we've got a lot to do.
Daffy: This is gonna be great!
Knick (as they exit): Hey, wait for me!

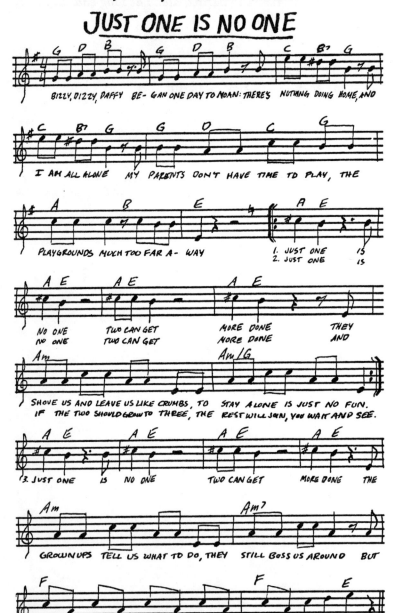

REPEAT AND FADE

JUST ONE   IS   NO ONE

YOURS OR MINE

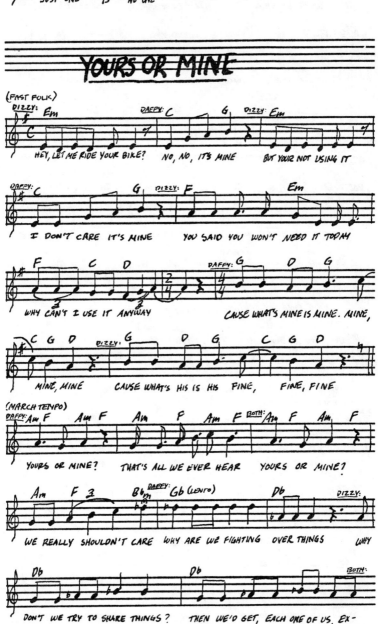

(FAST FOLK)

DIZZY: DAFFY: DIZZY:

HEY, LET ME RIDE YOUR BIKE?   NO, NO, IT'S MINE   BUT YOUR NOT USING IT

DAFFY: DIZZY:

I DON'T CARE IT'S MINE   YOU SAID YOU WON'T NEED IT TODAY

DAFFY:

WHY CAN'T I USE IT ANYWAY   CAUSE WHAT'S MINE IS MINE. MINE,

DIZZY:

MINE, MINE   CAUSE WHAT'S HIS IS HIS   FINE,   FINE, FINE

(MARCH TEMPO)

DAFFY: BOTH:

YOURS OR MINE?   THAT'S ALL WE EVER HEAR   YOURS OR MINE?

DAFFY: (LENTO)   DIZZY:

WE REALLY SHOULDN'T CARE   WHY ARE WE FIGHTING   OVER THINGS   WHY

BOTH:

DON'T WE TRY TO SHARE THINGS?   THEN WE'D GET, EACH ONE OF US, EX-

JUST WHAT WE NEED   THEN WE'D GET, EACH ONE OF US   JUST WHAT WE NEED.

ORDER MAKES UP HALF YOUR LIFE

(SWING TEMPO)

1. OH THE EVIL TIMES   ARE COMING   YOU CAN SEE THE PRO-
2. OH THE BOYS AND   GIRLS TODAY   DON'T KNOW OR WANT TO

BLEMS MOUNTING   THERE'S NO RESPECT AT ALL   NO MORE
    OBEY   THEY'RE ALWAYS ASKING   QUESTIONS

THE KIDS NOW ACT LIKE   OUT LAWS   SO WE NEED SOME LAW
AND WE DON'T HAVE SUG- GESTIONS   THEY DON'T HAVE MANNERS

AND ORDER   TO KEEP OUR COUN- TRY CLEAN   WHO'S THE MOST IM-
OR RESPECT   THE WHOLE WORLD'S GOING TO THE DOGS   WHO'S SUPPOSED TO

PORTANT, THEN?   ITS   US, OF COURSE, THE   LAW MEN
CHECK THIS, THEN?   ITS   US, OF COURSE, THE

FOR ORDER MAKES   UP HALF YOUR LIFE, WITHOUT ORDER, THE ENTIRE

EARTH WOULD CRUMBLE   KEEP ORDER,   AND ORDER WILL KEEP YOU

WITHOUT ORDER, ORDER WOULD BECOME DISORDER   ONLY THOSE WHO LOVE ORDER AND

CLEANLINESS   WILL   GET FAR   AND IT'S   ONLY THOSE   WHO

LOVE ORDER AND CLEANLINESS   WHO'LL BE A REAL SUCCESS.

LAW MEN

WHOEVER SAYS GIRLS ARE DUMB

(GUITAR)

1 WHOEVER SAYS GIRLS ARE DUMB
WHOEVER SAYS GIRLS ARE SCAREDYCATS

WHOEVER SAYS GIRLS JUST ACT SILLY   WHOEVER SAYS GIRLS ARE SHY   HAS
WHOEVER SAYS THEY'RE CRY BABIES   AND ALWAYS GRUMBLE AND COMPLAIN

GOT   NO BRAINS   NO BRAINS   BRAINS AT ALL

GIRLS ARE JUST AS SILLY AS BOYS   GIRLS ARE JUST AS FRESH AND

QUICK AND SMART GIRLS ARE JUST AB BRAVE AND STRONG AS BOYS

AND THEY CAN ALSO TAKE A - LOT

2. WHOEVER SAYS GIRLS ARE WEAK

~~WHOEVER SAYS GIRLS JUST ACT GOOFY~~
~~WHOEVER SAYS GIRLS ARE ZANY~~
~~HAS GOT NO BRAINS! NO BRAINS!~~

WHOEVER SAYS GIRLS ARE SISSIES
ARE TATTLETALES AND TROUBLESOME
AND MAKE MISTAKES BECAUSE THEY'RE DUMB
~~HAS GOT NO BRAINS! NO BRAINS AT ALL~~

ALL THE SONGS IN "BIZZY, DIZZY, DAFFY AND
ARTHUR" WERE WRITTEN BY;

WORDS: VOLKER LUDWIG
MUSIC: BIRGER HEYMANN
TRANSLATED FROM ORIGINAL GERMAN: JACK ZIPES
MUSIC ADAPTED: ANNE WARREN

MAN OH MAN

Original title: *Mannomann!* by Volker Ludwig and Reiner Lücker.
English translation by Jack Zipes.

Characters:

Christy
Pete
Mary Lou
Sue Roberts, Mother
Mac Herman, Father
Mr. Hambone, Landlord
Mrs. Snoop, Neighbor   } can be played by one actor
Salesman
Mr. Sneak, Foreman

Note: The Berlin production took place in a small arena. Three stages were used at different times. At the ends of the arena, there were two elevated stages where the street, kitchen, factory, and store scenes were played. The largest stage was set in the middle, three steps lower than the other two, and it was used only as the living room.

Mary Lou (*hops across the stage carrying her doll. She talks aloud in a sing-song manner*):

My daddy goes working
and makes all the money.
My daddy's my hero,
and me, I'm his honey.

My mommy does the cooking.
My mommy also sews.
She washes and mends.
She loves all she does.

I'm still very little,
but soon I'll be big.
And I'll be just like mommy
with a house full of kids.

My husband, he'll go working,
and I'll stay at home.
I know that I'll like this.
My mommy told me so.

(*Christy and Pete come running across the stage.*)
Christy: Last one to the corner is a rotten egg! On your mark, get set, go!
(*She takes off, bumps into Mary Lou, whose doll falls to the ground.*)
Mary Lou: Ohhh! My baby! (*She consoles her doll.*)

Christy and Pete quarrel about who won the race. They begin wrestling but are not serious. Both are obviously enjoying themselves even though Mary Lou thinks that they are really fighting.

Pete: No fair! You cheated!

Mary Lou: Hey, watch out!

Christy: I won! I won fair and square!

Pete: Like fun you did! You started before me!

Christy: That's what you think! I'm just faster than you!

Pete: You nuts or something? Boys are always faster than girls. Isn't that right, Mary Lou?

Mary Lou: Well, I guess so.

(*Pete and Christy laugh.*)

Pete: That's why you guys always have to cheat.

Mary Lou: Not me!

Christy: Well, what should we do? (*She gives her brother a punch. He goes on the defensive. She lands one in the bread basket.*)

Pete (*doubles up*): I won't fight with girls...

Mary Lou (*anxiously*): Christy, you better stop, otherwise he'll really get mad and let you have it...

Christy: Are you kidding? Just let him try it! (*pushes him.*)

Pete: O.K. if that's the way you want it. (*He attacks Christy.*)

Mary Lou: You see!

(*Hambone, the landlord, enters.*)

Christy: Only cowards attack from behind!

Hambone: Let go of that poor girl, you brat!

Pete: Why should I? That *poor, poor* girl started it all.

(*Christy pulls a reverse on Pete and has him down on his back.*)

Hambone: You kids! You've got the makings of hoodlums!

Christy: Who asked for your advice?

Hambone: What kind of a way is that to talk to a grown-up? You can be glad that I arrived in time or else you would have gotten quite a licking.

Christy (*smacks Pete*): Or else he would have!

(*Christy and Pete laugh. They scuffle.*)

Hambone: Now cut that out! Good girls don't roughhouse!

(*Pete pulls himself together and becomes serious.*)

Mary Lou: C'mon, Christy, let's go play with my doll.

Hambone: You see, your little friend here knows how to behave.

Pete: Will you clear out and leave us alone!

Christy: We don't tell you how to run your life.

(*Mother, Sue Roberts, enters.*)

Mother: Well, what's going on here? Have you two been up to something again?

Pete: He's the one who started everything, mom.

Mother (*recognizes Hambone*): Oh, Mr. Hambone. I apologize. The children are sometimes a bit wild.... What happened here?

Hambone: Are these your children, Mrs. Roberts?

Mother: Yes, these two.

Hambone: Well now, that doesn't make the matter any easier.

Christy: What do you mean?

Pete: Nothing happened!

Mary Lou: I was just standing here peacefully minding my own business.

Hambone: Yes, *you* were. You were the only one.

Mother: What's it all about?

Hambone: It concerns your rent, Mrs. Roberts. What else did you expect? And the situation is not very rosy for a single woman with two children like you. I want to be quite frank with you from the very beginning!

Mother: Would you like to come in for a moment?

The following sequence takes place alternatingly in two areas. Pete, Christy, and Mary Lou remain outside while Hambone and the mother are in the living room.

Pete: What's his name? Hambone or Chickenbone?

Christy: You clown!

Pete: Who is that guy anyway?

Christy: Must be our landlord or something like that.

Mary Lou: Oh-oh, that's trouble....Now you'll have to get out of your apartment because of what you did.

Christy: We haven't done a thing!

* * * * *

Hambone (*takes some papers out of a briefcase*): Well now, Mrs. Roberts, I have the unpleasant task of informing you that the building in which you're living will be torn down in five months.

Mother: What?

* * * * *

Mary Lou: Come on, Christy. Boys are too silly. Let's play house together.

* * * * *

Mother: Yes, but Mr. Ham...

Hambone: Now, don't get upset, Mrs. Roberts. Naturally we'll provide another apartment for you. In fact, it'll be in one of those new developments. Here are the application forms.

Mother: In a new development. But what will that cost?!

* * * * *

Pete: How can you play house? You need a father, mother and baby, and there are only two of you!

Mary Lou: That's not true at all! You forgot about Topsy. (*She points to her doll.*)

* * * * *

Hambone: Of course, it'll be a bit more expensive. I'll grant you that. The rent should come to about two hundred dollars a month.

Mother: Two hundred dollars a month? That's double what we're paying now. How can I afford that?

* * * * *

Christy: Let Pete play the father.

Mary Lou: No... Boys have their own games, and we have ours.

* * * * *

Hambone: You don't have to move there, you know. No one's particularly anxious to have you and your kids around anyway. But one thing's certain: you'll have to get out of here!

Mother: And what if I can't pay the new rent?

Hambone: That's your affair.

* * * * *

Pete: But you need a boy to play the father!

Mary Lou: You mean you really want to play with dolls?!

Christy: Forget the doll! You'll be the child, and you the father, and I'll be the mother.

* * * * *

Hambone: Why don't you get married again? If you had a husband, he'd earn enough money so that you'd be able to pay the new rent. And then the children could also learn some manners.

Mother: That's my affair, Mr. Hambone!

Hambone leaves the apartment and heads down the street toward the children. He doesn't watch where he's going and bumps into one of them.

Hambone: Will you watch where you're going? What do you think the street is, a playground? (*Exits. The children stare after him in amazement.*)

Mary Lou: O.K. We'll do it your way. Now, that'll be our living room, and there's the tv.

Pete: I'll sit here in my easy chair.

Mary Lou: Daddy's watching tv, and we have to be very quiet. So, I'll play with Topsy, and you have to sew.

Christy: But I want to watch tv, too.

Mary Lou: O.K. You can do that, but you also have to sew while you watch. That's the way my mommy always does it.

Christy (*chants*): Sew, sew, sew...

Mary Lou: Daddy—?

Pete: Yes, honey.

Mary Lou: Wrong! You've got to yell—"Quiet! Don't bother me!"

Pete: Quiet! Don't bother me!

Mary Lou: Now, once more, and this time, do it right!

Christy: Sew, sew, sew...

Mary Lou: Daddy—?

Pete: Quiet! Don't bother me!

Mary Lou: And now: "Hey, where the hell's my beer?!"

Pete: Hey, where the hell's my beer?!

Christy: How should I know? I'm watching tv.

Mary Lou: Wrong! You've got it all wrong! You've got to say: "I'm sorry, dear. I'll get it for you right away." And then you run into the kitchen.

Christy: Hey, do you really think that mothers as dumb as this exist in real life?

Mary Lou: My mother isn't dumb! The only reason you guys can't play the game the right way is because you don't have a daddy.

Pete: Well, we don't need a stupid daddy like this one...

Christy: Anyway, we're not going to play if you're always giving the orders!

Mary Lou: But this is the way you're supposed to play house!

Pete: O.K. Then, let's do it your way....So, now I yell: "Get going. Off to the kitchen, and hurry it up!"

Christy: Hey, who do you think you are, a king or something?

Pete: Shut your mouth!

(*Christy kicks him in the shins. They scuffle.*)

Mary Lou: Darn it, Christy! You always have to spoil things. If you're gonna be the mommy, then you've got to do what the daddy says. —I'm gonna play with Topsy by myself since you guys can't follow the rules. Topsy always does what I want to do. She's my little bundle of joy, aren't you Topsy? (*Exits. Nearly in tears.*)

Christy: What does she think? Fathers aren't supposed to be howling apes...It would be nice to have a daddy...but not one like that....

Pete: That's the way Mary Lou's father is.

Christy: You think mom would put up with a grouch like that?

Pete: If she were married, she'd have to, most likely.

Christy: Man oh man! You're crazy...(*Sings.*)

> I'd like to have a daddy.
> It'd really be quite nice.
> A man at home who'd fight for us,
> a man we'd all support.
>
> But a father who just screams—Man oh man!
> Who rants and raves and steams—Man oh man!
> Who only watches tv—Man oh man!
> Who won't let anyone be free—Man oh man!

How do you deal with someone like that?
Man oh man oh man oh man oh man!

Man oh man, man oh man,
Women do all the dirty work,
all the junk and all the slop,
always mopping up.

Man oh man, man oh man,
Men never lend a hand.
But if one shouts, watch out!
That really stinks!

Both: Man oh man, man oh man,
let's all work now hand in hand.
Girls and boys, moms and dads,
we're all the same.

And whoever starts again
to say that we're not the same
and fights against our aims
just has no brains!

Man oh man, man oh man,
let's all work now hand in hand.
Girls and boys, moms and dads,
we're all the same.

II

Breakfast

*The scene must show that most of the work is shared and that
an atmosphere of friendliness and cooperation prevails despite
the fact that things are hectic and there is no father.*

Christy: Good morning! Pete, hurry up! Mom's got to get to work.

Pete: All right, already. —Do you know where my arithmetic notebook is? (*He looks in Christy's school bag.*)

Christy (*laughing*): Hey, get out of there. —It's your turn to get the doughnuts.

Pete: But I won't have time if I have to look for my notebook. Mom, do you know where I put my notebook?

Mother (*from the kitchen*): It's on top of the tv.

Pete: Oh, there it is. . . . Well, I guess I'll have to go get the doughnuts.

Christy: Hey, don't forget to take some money. . . . Oh, you sleepyhead, I'd better run and do it. Get your things together. Mom, can I buy some ice cream, too?

Mother: No, you'd better not. The prices have just gone up, and we've got to watch our budget! (*Christy exits. Mother enters.*) Now where did I put my wallet? Christy!

Pete: She already left.

Mother: Have you seen my wallet?

Pete: Christy took it with her.

Mother: Oh, you're not finished setting the table yet. (*She helps Pete.*)

Pete: That's because I couldn't find my notebook.

Mother: I know. You'd lose your head if it weren't attached to you.

Pete: What do you mean? I never even knew it was attached to me in the first place.

Mother (*laughs*): Hey, you'd better tell Christy to get some margarine.

Pete: But she already left.

Mother: Well, shout to her from the window, otherwise there'll be no breakfast for you.

Pete (*runs to the window*): Chriiiisty!! Don't forget to buy some margarine!!! (*Returns.*) Oh-oh, I forgot the eggs.

Mother: Bring the jam in, too.

Pete: O.K. O.K. (*Goes into the kitchen.*) Mom, can we go swimming, today? (*He returns with the eggs.*)

Mother: I'm afraid not, Pete. Not today. That's what I wanted to tell you before....Where's the jam??

Pete: Oh, jeeze, I forgot it. (*Returns to the kitchen.*)

Christy (*enters*): Hey mom, mom!

Mother: What's that you've got there?

Christy: A ten dollar bill! Here. Now we can buy some extra stuff like ice cream!

Mother: Where'd you find it?

Christy: On the stairs.

Pete (*coming from the kitchen*): Did someone lose it?

Christy: Sure! What do you think?

Mother (*happy*): Really?

Christy: Yeah! I even saw the woman who was looking for it.

Mother (*sighs*): Christy! Return the money immediately!!

Christy: But I'm sure she was looking for something else...

Mother (*warning her*): Christy!

Christy: I'll get the salt.

Mother: The salt's here.

Christy: Then I'll get the vacuum cleaner. Or the—the—sewing machine. Well, what do you want me to get?

Mother: Christy, whose money is that?

Christy: I don't know. I found it. Of course, I did see Mrs. Snoop on the stairs looking for something. But maybe her teeth fell out. She's always losing her teeth, you know.

Mother: Now, you go right to Mrs. Snoop and ask her whether she lost the ten dollars.

(*The doorbell rings.*)

Mother: Can't we eat breakfast in peace?

(*Christy and Pete race to the door to see who can get there first.*)

Pete: You know something? (*Stops Christy.*)

Christy: What?

Pete: I think the doorbell rang! (*He goes to the door and opens it a crack.*) It's Mrs. Snoop.

Snoop (*pushes the door open*): I must speak to your poor mother right away. (*Storms past the children.*)

Christy: Why is our mother so poor?

Pete: She didn't even say good morning!

Mother: Oh, be quiet now and sit down.

Pete: Well, I'm not gonna say good morning to her anymore either.

Mrs. Snoop: Well then, Mrs. Roberts, what in heaven's name is the matter with you? Even a single woman should be able to raise her children so that—so that....

Mother: Well?

Snoop: I'll break my neck for sure if you let your children run around like wild animals! —Mmmmmmm—I smell fresh coffee, don't I? Well, if you insist, I guess I can drink a tiny cup with you, but just a tiny cup! (*She sits down.*)

Mother: Excuse me, but I've got to go to work.

Snoop: That's just it. If you have children, you shouldn't be away the entire day working. Well, you'll see.... At any rate, you've got to get out of here!

Mother: You, too. The building's going to be torn down this winter.

Snoop: Who told you that?!

Christy: Wishbone!

Pete: Bonehead!

Mother: Mr. Hambone, the landlord. Now, I really must go.

Snoop: So. —But one thing you don't know is that there are very few new buildings and only quiet tenants get first choice on the apartments there. I'm on very good terms with Caspar Hambone, and just yesterday he asked me: my dear Emily, he asked, do you think that Mrs. Roberts and her children would make good tenants in the new development? And my answer was: you know how it is, Mr. Hambone, you know how it is...So, I didn't say no. But without a husband and with children like yours...What can I tell you, Mrs. Roberts? What would you have said if you had been in my shoes?

Mother: Well, I'm going now. Are you coming?

Snoop: At least let me finish my cup of coffee. So then, as I was saying...

Christy: You sneak all over the house and tell Bonehead everything you hear.

Mother: Christy! Tell Mrs. Snoop you're sorry. Right now!

Christy: Well, I'm sorry, but that's the way it looks to me.

Snoop: What? How can you say such a thing? I tell you, Mrs. Roberts, until now I was ready to put in a good word or two for you. But your children are already so far gone that I'll not lift a finger for you. These brats belong in a home! Oh dear, my heart! I've had enough excitement for today. Just a little while ago I lost ten dollars.

Christy: On the stairs?

Mrs. Snoop: That's right! You didn't see it, did you?

Christy: If it was a ten dollar bill, I think I saw it somewhere. (*She runs outside with Mrs. Snoop following her.*)

Pete: What kind of a ten dollar bill was it?

Snoop: A green one!

Christy: There it is! (*She comes back in, points outside. Mrs. Snoop runs outside. Christy slams the door shut.*) Well, we finally got rid of her.

Mother: That takes care of that. Now I've got to get going. Oh—so don't forget. Do me a favor and don't go swimming today. I'd also appreciate it if you cleaned up a bit. I invited someone to drop by and won't have time to clean after I do the shopping. Bye now.

Pete: Who's coming over?

Mother: A man I know at the factory.

Christy: Have you known him for a long time?

Mother: Pretty long. Look, I've got to rush now. So long. . . . And don't forget to clean up. (*Exits.*)

Christy: A man!

Pete: Hmmm. A man's coming over, and just because of that she doesn't want us to go swimming.

Christy: That's never happened before!. . .C'mon, we've got to head for school.

Pete: We've got to clear the table first.

Christy: Ooops, I almost forgot. (*They clean up.*)

Pete and Christy (*while cleaning up*):

> Man oh man, man oh man,
> let's all work now hand in hand.
> Girls and boys, moms and dads,
> we're all the same.

Man oh man, man.........

III

The Visit

The room is in a mess. Pete and Christy are on the floor playing with racing cars.

(*Mary Lou rings the bell.*)

Christy: It's open!

Mary Lou: Hey, how come you guys didn't go swimming with us?

Pete (*stops playing*): We've got to clean up.

Christy: Some man's coming over to visit us.

Mary Lou: But you haven't cleaned a thing.

Christy: We've got plenty of time. Mom won't be home for another hour.

Pete: Say, Mary Lou, you don't have to go home for awhile, do you?

Mary Lou: Nahhh...

Pete (*jumps up*): That's perfect! Then you two can do the cleaning up!

Christy: You're off your rocker!

Pete: I'll give you something for it—some bubble gum.

Christy: No way!

Mary Lou: Bubble gum? For the both of us...(*Pete nods.*) Then let's do it, Christy. Boys don't know how to clean anyway. They're too clumsy.

Pete: That's right. They just knock everything over! (*He knocks some notebooks off the table.*) You see?

Mary Lou: You did that on purpose!

Christy: Boy, are you smart!!

Pete: I don't even know where things belong.

Christy: You think I do?

Mary Lou: When someone comes to visit us, we have to clean up, too. My daddy always wants everything nice and neat. And my mommy says that the only way I'll ever marry later on when I grow up is if I learn to cook and clean house.

Christy: Well, then I'm gonna stay a widow for the rest of my life. (*They throw a table cloth over Mary Lou's head and turn her around in circles.*)

Mother (*enters, is speechless, then yells*): Have you gone crazy?! (*They stop. The table cloth falls to the ground. Mother sets down a bag of food.*)

Mary Lou: It wasn't my fault, Mrs. Roberts. I wanted to help Christy clean up, but Pete, he—

Mother: I especially asked you to clean up today because someone's coming over. What do you want Mac to think of me?

Christy: Mac? Who's Mac?

Mother (*who has calmed down*): I told you, my friend. The one who works in the factory. He'll be coming over soon.

Pete: How come you're home so early?

Mother: Because...because I wanted to get things ready. Now, may I clean up!

Mary Lou: I'll help you, Mrs. Roberts.

Christy: You've never yelled at us like this before....

Mother: I'm a little on edge. Forget it, will you?

Mary Lou: We understand!

Pete: Butt out, dummy! We'll take care of everything, mom! (*The doorbell rings. Mother jumps nervously.*)

Mother: My God! It's Mac!

Pete: Already?

Mary Lou: I'll get it.

Mother: Oh no, and I'm not even ready! (*Primps her hair quickly. The doorbell rings again.*)

Christy: He's a real eager beaver, isn't he?

Mother: Bring these things into the kitchen. (*She gives Christy the groceries. Christy exits.*)

Salesman (*outside*): Good day! Is your mother at home?

Mary Lou: No, she lives in the next building, up one flight. I'll take you to her if you want me to.

Pete: Man, are you nuts or something? (*Runs to the door.*) Of course she's here. She's been waiting for you!

Salesman: Is it all right if I come in?

Pete: You're already in.

Mother: What can I do for you?

Salesman: Sorry for the disturbance, m'am but I just want to present you with this small gift, and then I'll leave immediately.

Mother: Well, what is it?

Pete: You mean that's not the guy.

Mother: Oh, c'mon, you know me better than that.

Salesman (*pulls out some magazines from a briefcase*): Here's *The Beautiful World of Women*—I'm sure you've heard of it!

Mother: No.

Salesman: Well, then a woman like you just has to get to know *The Beautiful World of Women*! My customers have assured me that they owe more to *The Beautiful World of Women* than their own fathers, doctors, husbands—and even their lovers!

Mother: Please go now. I really have...

Salesman: Everything that the modern woman must know is in here. How to make herself beautiful for the man she loves, how men want to be entertained, how to make the home fit his taste, what he likes to eat, his innermost secrets—all this is revealed for you by *The Beautiful World of Women*. (*Christy enters.*) *The Beautiful World of Women* knows what men desire.

Christy: But that's one of those women's magazines!

Salesman: Right you are, little girl. The housewife's best friend!

Christy: So why do they write about what *men* desire?

Salesman: Aha, well, men live for their work, and women live for their men. Isn't that right, m'am?

Christy: What a load of junk!

Salesman: Charming child....Now, all you have to do is sign here, and you'll receive *The Beautiful World* every Wednesday....afterall, you do want to be up to date, radical chic, in fashion, don't you? I'm sure that....

Mother: Will you go now! I don't have any money to waste on things like this!

Salesman: You can pay later....You're just the person for a magazine like this....

Mother: If you don't go right now, I'll call the police.

Pete: Right on, mom! Want me to do it?

Mary Lou: I just don't know why you're all getting so upset! He's really a nice man...Hey, mister, do you want to see my mommy?

Salesman: Love to, my dear child, I'd love to! (*Turns to Mrs. Roberts.*) You can think it over.

Mary Lou: I'll take you there, O.K.?

Salesman (*grabs the free copy he gave the mother*): Let's go, little girl. You lead the way. (*Exits with Mary Lou.*)

Pete: Hey, that's our free copy!

Mother (*begins to put on make-up and get ready*): Christy, will you hang this coat up?

Christy: Sure. (*Exits.*)

Pete (*goes to his mother's side and looks at her*): How come you're getting so dolled up, mom?

Mother: Because someone's coming to visit me.

Pete: Is it because he's a man?

Mother: No, not really.

Pete: Well then, how come you don't put on make-up when Aunt Elly comes to visit us?

Mother: She doesn't like make-up.

Pete: How do you know that the man who's coming over likes make-up?

Mother: All men like make-up.

Pete: So you are putting on make-up because a man's visiting us. You want him to be attracted to you, right?

Mother: No—I'm doing it because I look pretty this way.

Pete: Why are you making yourself look so pretty? You never do it for us.

Mother: Because....because all men like women to look pretty.

Pete: So that fast-talking salesman was right: women only do what men want!?

Mother: No, Pete, you've got it all wrong. I enjoy it, too...

Pete: Well, why don't men wear make-up? Why only women?

Mother: How should I know?

Pete: I know! Because men are naturally handsome and women aren't. So they have to put on all this make-up junk so that men will be attracted to them. Right?

Mother: C'mon now, stop this nonsense.

Christy (comes from the kitchen): Look at this! Mr. Fast-talker forgot his lid.

(*The doorbell rings.*)

Mother: That's probably him. Go and give it to him.

Pete (grabs the hat from Christy): I'll do it! (*He opens the door a crack and shoves the hat through.*) Here, take your moth-eaten hat and scram! (*He slams the door shut.*)

(*The doorbell rings again. The children giggle.*)

Mother: Will you two cut it out and open the door!

Pete: I already did.

Mother (is mad, crosses the floor in a housecoat, and rips the door open): Now you stop bothering us or else I'll really call...Mac! (*Mac stands outside with the hat on his head, roses in the left hand and a ball and a doll under the right arm.*)

Mother: Oh Mac! It's you already—I thought—Oh, never mind—come in, come in.

Mac (enters. His eyes are glued on her. So, he doesn't see the stairs and falls down them. From a sitting position): You want to explain the bit with the hat to me?

Mother: Oh, Pete thought—you see, there was a salesman here before who forgot his hat—Listen, I'd better finish changing.

Mac (standing): First, let me give you this. (*Hands her the flowers.*)

Mother: Oh, Mac, that wasn't necessary. Really! Well, I'll leave you all alone for a second. (*Exits.*)

Mac: So, you're Christy. Here I brought you something! (*He gives her the doll.*) And this is for Pete! (*He throws him the football.*)

Pete and Christy: Thanks!

Pete: Hey, you're all right!

Christy (*drops the doll*): Oh, a football! (*They start playing football and practically ignore Mac.*)

Mac: Errr....So now....I'm your Uncle Mac...The doll's for you, Christy.

Christy: Yeah, I know. Thanks. (*Keeps playing football.*)

Mac: Well then, should we...uh...Pete, you interested in cars?

Pete (*stops playing with Christy*): Sure. What kind of a car you have?

Mac: Just call me Uncle Mac. A Pinto...

Pete: Oh, one of those small cars.

Mac: Yeah, but it's a souped-up job.

Pete: Really!? But I thought a Pinto...

Mac: This is a special make. It's used for rallies. Almost like a racing car.

Pete: No kidding!...How fast can it go?

(*Christy is bored and exits.*)

Mac: You guess. Go on. Guess!

Pete: A hundred miles an hour.

Mac: It does a hundred with ease!

Pete: Wheww! (*falls off his chair and begins to play racing car driver with his chair.*) Rum-rum-rum, rum-rum-rum!

Mother (*returns with the flowers in a vase*): Well, have you all got to know each other a little?...Will you stand up?

(*Mac jumps up out of his seat.*)

Mother: No, not you! Pete, get off the floor!

Pete: Hey, mom, he's got a car that'll...

Mother: Who's he? His name is—

Mac: Mac. Call me Uncle Mac.

Pete: Mom, he's got one of these small cars, but it can do a hundred.

Mother: That's terrific!

Christy (comes out of the kitchen): I'm supposed to ask you if you want some beer.

Mac: Well, now that you're asking, I wouldn't mind a small glass, but just a small one.

(Christy exits.)

Pete: Tell me, have you ever driven in a race?

Mac: Of course I have. All kinds of races. You name it!.... Maybe we'll take a drive together on the weekend. What do you say about that?

Mother: That'll make you happy, won't it?

Christy (brings a can of beer): Here you are.

Mother: Where's the glass?

Mac: Thanks, Christy, thanks. Forget it. I'll drink it out of the can. *(To Christy.)* Tell me, how old are you?

Pete: You tell us how old you are first.

Mother: Pete, you're not supposed to ask such questions...

Christy: Why not? He asked me, didn't he?

Mac: Well, I'm thirty-two. No, wait a minute. I'm thirty-one.

Christy: You're that old!

(Mac laughs in embarrassment.)

Pete: Now tell us how come you're here.

Mother: But, Pete, I invited Mac just to stop over and spend some time with us.

Mac: That's right. Besides that, I like your mother.

Christy: Where'd you get to know him, Mom?

Mother: We work in the same firm.

Christy: Does he pack light bulbs like you?

Mother: No, no, Mac earns much more money....

Mac: I drive a fork lift in the delivery department.

Pete: A fork lift? What does it do, lift forks?

Mac (laughs): No, you know the ones that lift up large crates and carry them to trucks or storage rooms.

Christy: How d'you drive one of those things?

Mac: Well, it's like this. I sit there on this special seat. There's an electric motor underneath it. In front there are these two long iron slats which come down to the floor and form a kind of a fork underneath. Then the fork gets under the crates and lifts them—bzzzzz, bzzzzzz, then I drive the crates to another spot and lower the fork with the crates—wrrrrrr, wrrrrrr. —It's simple.

Christy (pretends to drive the fork lift): Why can't mommy drive the fork lifts? Then she'd earn more money!

Mac (whispers the answer softly to their mother): Only men can drive fork lifts.

Mother: Only men can drive fork lifts.

Pete: You've got to be real strong for that, huh?

Mac: That's it! No, come to think of it, everything's electric.

Christy: So how come only men are allowed to drive the cars.

Mother: That's just the way things are.

Mac: Because—it's real complicated.

Christy: Couldn't women learn how to drive one of them?

Mac: I'm not sure...but that wouldn't interest women anyway.

Christy: I don't think that's fair at all.

Mother: Oh, let's talk about something else.

Pete: And why doesn't mom get as much money as you?

Mac: She does something else.

Christy: Men always get more money than women even when they do the exact same job. You told us that yourself, mom!

Mac: Women should spend more time looking after the children...

Christy: I know why that's the way it is: because all the bosses are men, and men always give other men more than they give women. Man oh man, it's really a man's world!

Mac: Oh yeah, what would you two say if your mother didn't have to work so much anymore?

Pete and Christy: That'd be great!

Mother: And—Pete, you've always wanted a father, right?

Pete: Sure.

Mother: And you, too, Christy? Right?

Christy: Yeah, that's right....but why you asking such wierd questions, mom?

Pete: I bet I know. You want to marry Uncle Mac!

Mother: That's it.

Mac: Uh....your mom and me...I'd like to...what I want

to say...

Mother: We want to get married. Then I'd only work half a day as a waitress or something, and afternoons I'd be at home with you. How do you like that?

Christy: Don't know. It all depends on how he is.

(*The doorbell rings.*)

Pete (*runs to the door and opens it*): It's that fast-talking salesman again!

Salesman (*enters the room*): Excuse me, but I had a—yes there it is. My hat. (*Pete hands him the hat.*) Aha, you have a visitor, m'am. —How'd you like to buy a subscription to *The Beautiful World of Women* for your lady friend? You won't regret it. (*He continues to give them the fast sell.*)

Mother (*interrupting him*): I told you before that I don't want to subscribe... I buy magazines around the corner at the candy store when I want them....Mac, will you please tell him to go.

Mac (*approaches the salesman*): Hey, buddy, if you don't move your tail out of here in two seconds flat, then you'll be selling magazines from a hospital bed. Now get out of my apartment!

Salesman: But I was only asking... (*He flees in panic. They all stare in admiration at the new lord of the house.*)

IV

Three Months Later

(*Late afternoon. Father and mother are at home.*)

Father (*walks in*): Well, it's the same old story. For once I'd like to come home from work and see supper on the table.

Mother: Oh, Mac, c'mon. How am I supposed to know when you come home from work.

Father: We've been married over three months. You should

know by now that I get off work at 4:30.

Mother: And sometimes you have a beer with the boys, and then I have to re-heat everything so that you can have a hot meal.

Father: Now don't you start in with your stories of how hard you work in the kitchen. Where're the kids? I'm hungry.

Mother: They should be here any second. If you would only help a bit instead of just grumbling about everything, then dinner'd already be on the table.

Father: That's all I need. I break my back the entire day, for all of you, and then I'm supposed to come home and play housewife.

Mother: And me, what do you think I do the entire day, live it up? From eight until one, I work in the restaurant. Then I come home and have to take care of everything here. But I guess you don't call this work!

Father: You know you can't compare what you do with my work. I'm going all day long. That takes a lot out of you.

Mother: I thought you drove a fork lift?

Father: What do you know about my work? Once you start earning as much as I do, then you can start talking. Now, I want something to eat, damn it!

(*The three children enter.*)

Pete: Hi, dad.

Christy: Hi, Mom.

Mary Lou: Hi, everybody.

(*Mother goes into the kitchen.*)

Father: Where've you been? Can't you be here on time for supper?

Pete: Supper's not even ready yet.

Father: That's just it! If you two would help, then I wouldn't have to sit around here and wait for it!

Christy: Maybe you could help mom for a change instead of just sitting around.

Father: You go into the kitchen and help out so we can eat. Now get a move on!...Are you also snotty to your father, Mary Lou?

Mary Lou (*laughs in embarrassment*): No? Noo! Never....I

like to help out at home, and daddy always says that I'll be the perfect housewife.

Father: Why don't you sit down. Well, Christy will learn to become one, too. She grew up too long without a father...She doesn't even play with dolls.

Mary Lou: Well, sometimes we play house together.

Father: You know something. I think you're a good friend for Christy. She can learn a lot from you!

Pete: Christy is one of the best football players on the block. Why does she have to learn to play with dolls?

Father: Who asked you? Come here. Run over to the grocer's and buy me a six pack of beer!

Pete: Can I get some ice cream, too?

Father: You had ice cream yesterday.

Pete: You had beer yesterday.

Father: Now that's enough of that! Do I have to teach you a lesson?

Pete: I get enough of that in school. (*Exits*)

Mother (*comes in with the dinner*): Well, we can eat now. Do you want to join us, Mary Lou?

Mary Lou: No, thank you, Mrs. Herman. I've eaten already.

Mother: Where's Pete?

Father: He went to get me some beer.

Mother: Do you always have to send him for something when we're just about to eat?

Father: If you would make sure there's beer in the house, then this wouldn't happen!

Mother: You could easily help with the shopping. You have a car. And now that I think of it, you even promised to help me out today. Then you could have bought a whole case of beer.

Father: There's a football game on tv tonight.

Christy: But you have a car. You could go after dinner. It only takes a second, and then nobody has to lug all the stuff.

Father: You keep out of this. It doesn't concern you.

Christy: Sure it concerns me.

Father: Quiet! Stop bothering me! I'm losing my appetite.

Mary Lou: My mother always goes shopping alone. She says

that men are always a big nuisance in the store because they're always mixing in.

(*Pete comes with the beer.*)

Mother: Come eat. We're almost finished.

Father: You could have put a little more meat in this casserole, you know.

Mother: You could give me a little more money for food, you know!

Father: Your entire salary's supposed to cover all the shopping. That should be enough. My money goes for everything else.

Mother: I just make it with my money. So don't expect me to buy extra things.

Father: Christy, get me the salt.

Christy: Why do you always ask me?

Father: Get me the salt or else I'll really let you have it!

Christy: Aren't we in a good mood today?

(*Father makes threatening gestures.*)

Pete: I'll get it...

Father (to Christy): You go! —I have enough trouble at work, so I don't want anymore of this stinking nonsense at home. The foreman began yelling at me today, during the morning break. He said I piled some crates too high even though he was the one who told me to pile them five on top of the other. Five. Nothing less, nothing more. Well, you should've seen how I told him off. You'd better believe it! I won't let anyone order me around. Hear? And I won't put up with anyone mouthing off, and especially not at home. So knock off the back-talk and learn some respect! You hear?

Christy: Yeah, we hear.

Pete: We're finished now.

Christy: Can we go outside and play with Mary Lou?

Father: Yeah, take off, I've seen enough of you for today.

Christy: Let's go, Mary Lou.

Mary Lou: Bye-bye, Mr. Herman. Bye-bye, Mrs. Herman.

(*Father picks up the paper and begins reading it. The mother clears the table. The children head for the street.*)

V

On the Street

Pete: Man oh man, is he in a bad mood again!

Mary Lou: If you guys treated him better, then...

Christy: Don't be so dumb. I just don't see why he expects us all to serve him hand and foot.

Mary Lou: Don't tell me that you want your father to help with the housework?

Christy: Why not? Everyone can do a part of the housework.

Mary Lou: Men do housework! You're crazy. I'd like to see one father in the whole world who'd agree to do housework.

Pete: That might be pretty wierd.

Christy: Yeah, well they might learn a thing or two. Women work, too, you know. (*She raises and lowers her arms as if she were driving the fork lift.*)

Pete: Hey yeah, let's play loading with the fork lift.

Christy: I'm the fork lift.

Pete: And I'm the driver.

(*Both get ready to play their roles.*)

Christy: This is great. And we're unloading the circus.

Pete: A flea circus?

Christy: No dummy, you don't need a fork lift for that. The first thing we'll unload is a truck full of monkeys. It's over there.

(*Pete jumps around and pretends to be a monkey now.*)

Mary Lou: And what do I do?

Christy: You're his wife.

Mary Lou: The monkey's wife.

Christy: No, the driver's wife. (*She tells Pete to get ready.*) C'mon.

Mary Lou: Gee, this is terrific. I'll clean up everything at home for him. (*She begins to clean the floor.*)

Pete and Christy play loading and drive around. At one point, they miss signals and tumble to the ground.

Pete: Hey, that's not how it goes!

Christy: You're right.

Pete: Now the monkey's got away. (*He hops like a monkey to Mary Lou.*)

Mary Lou: Hey, that's my floor! Christy, get that monkey out of here. I just cleaned the floor! —I'm trying to make the house nice and neat for my husband. (*Christy drags Pete away.*)

Pete: I don't want to unload anymore. It's quitting time anyway. Time to go home. Where's my money?

Christy (*as boss counts out the money and places it in his hand*): 50, 100, 150, 200, 250.

(*Mary Lou comes over and holds out her hand, too.*)

Christy: Housewives don't get paid, dummy!

Mary Lou: What? Then, then I want to unload. I want to be the driver.

Christy: Good idea. Let's change.

Pete: O.K. But only for a short time. (*He begins to clean the floor reluctantly.*)

Mary Lou: And we'll unload the elephants.

Christy: Right! (*They drive off but in different directions.*) Hey, where are you going?

Mary Lou: The elephants are over here.

Christy: No, the elephants are here.

Mary Lou: Here!

Christy: Here?

Pete: Bong! Bong! Time to quit. Pick up your money.

Christy (*as boss*): Now where d'you say the elephants were?

Mary Lou (*meekly*): Wherever you say, boss.

Christy: 50, 100, 150, 200, 250. Wait a second, that's too much. 230, 210, 190. You don't get as much because you're a woman.

Pete: And I get more because I'm a man. And besides that, I spent the entire day on my hands and knees, and she only unloaded elephants.

Christy: That's what you think! You get nothing for housework
and that's final!

Pete: But that's not fair!

Christy: That's what I say, too!

Mary Lou: But my mommy gets some money. She saves
shopping coupons and blue chip stamps. (*She suddenly
freezes in her tracks.*)

Christy: The most she makes on that is a dollar or two for one
whole month of hard work. That's what I call a great
salary!

Mary Lou: Ughhhhh! I stepped in some dog du-du!

Pete: You mean elephant shit!

Mary Lou (*begins to jump around to clean her shoe. She then
runs home crying*): Momeee! Momeee!

Christy: What a character!

Pete: Oh, c'mon. Let her alone. Let's go play some football.
(*Both exit.*)

VI

In the Living Room

(*Father is reading the newspaper.*)

Mother (*comes out of the kitchen*): I'm going out tonight.

Father: What! Where are you going?

Mother: It doesn't matter where. You go out alone as often as
you want.

Father: Yeah, to play poker.

Mother: And I'm going bowling with Margie. I need some
money.

Father: Hey, you know what I think, I think you're not
yourself anymore, huh? A married woman don't go out
with another single woman at night to have a good time
while her husband pays for it and stays home.

Mother: First of all, we're only going bowling, and secondly, you're also married and you go to many places without me and have a good time.

Father: What do I do?

Mother: You know damn well. You take off whenever you want and spend plenty of money on yourself. And to tell you the truth, I don't like continually begging whenever I need just a little extra money for my own pleasure: (*She sings.*)

> I slave away the whole long day
> as housewife here and waitress there.
> My husband then comes home at six
> and sits like a king in his easy chair.

Father: Man, my work just knocks me out.
> So, I need peace or else I'll shout.

Mother: Ha! And me? I work like you.
> Plus, there's the housework I do.

Both: How do you deal with someone like her (him)?!
> Man oh man, man oh man!

Mother: Man oh man, man oh man,
> all the money that I earn
> is used so we can eat.
> I make ends meet.
> Man oh man, man oh man!
> There's not a cent to spare,
> and I help you out, too.
> But you don't care!

Father: But I earn three times more than you. — Man oh man!

Mother: That's not fair, and you know it, too. — Man oh man!

Father: My work is hard as hell —

Mother: Well I work much more and don't get paid.
> You only want me for your maid,
> cook, and washingwoman.
> Man oh man, man oh man! —

Father (*interrupts her by yelling*): Do you really want......?!
> Do you really want me to pay you for housework? Then I might as well get me a housekeeper. You're off your rocker! (*Exits*)

Pete (*still outside*): Man they're playing the super bowl on tv!

(*Pete and Christy run into the living room.*)

Pete: Hey mom, can we watch tv?

Mother: What about your homework?

Christy: Oh, we finished that a couple of hours ago.

Father (*enters and turns the tv on*): Now quiet. I don't want any noise in here. You've got some shopping to do, don't you? Take the kids with you to help out.

Pete: But I wanted to see the super bowl!

Father: Well, O.K. You can stay. But Christy, I want you to go with your mother.

Christy: But I wanted to see the game, too!

Father: What do you know about football?

Christy: As much as Pete does, that's for sure!

Pete: Come off it!

Father: Now you listen to me. I said that you go shopping with your mother, and that's the end of that!

Mother: We're not going shopping now. I want to read the newspaper in peace. I'll go shopping with you tomorrow, in the car.

Father: Man, do what you want! Just shut up for now! The game's about to begin!

Christy: Man, they're huge!

Pete: That's the Dolphins. They're the champs!

Christy: Wheww, I wouldn't want to get in that guy's way!

Father: Quiet!!

Mother: Where's today's paper?

Father: Man, it's in the bathroom where I put it. Where do you think? (*The commentator begins to talk.*) Hey, Sue, now that you're up, bring me some potato chips and a beer, huh?

Mother: Can't I rest for five minutes? (*She exits. The doorbell rings.*)

Father: Christy, go open the door.

Christy (*goes to the door*): It's Mr. Chickenbone!

Father: Christy!! (*He jumps from his seat.*) How are you, Mr. Hambone? Why don't you come in and sit down.

Hambone: Good evening, Mr. Herman. Thank you. Just stopped by for a minute. I won't stay long. Just want to report about the new apartment.

Father: Is something wrong?

Pete: Touchdown! Touchdown! Did you see that pass? (*Father turns down the tv. Pete and Christy move closer to the screen.*)

Hambone: Now then, there are some problems about your apartment.

Father: What's wrong now. If you tear this building down, then you've got to supply us with a new apartment. That's the law.

Hambone: Careful, careful now, Mr. Herman. You married Mrs. Roberts...

Father: Well, what do you have against that?

Hambone: Nothing. I'm happy that Mrs. Roberts is married again. That makes it much safer for all the tenants. A man in the house, good job, steady income. With single women, you never know—sometimes they have more children. You know how it is—mothers who work—somehow it's unnatural, don't you think so?

Father: Sure, sure. Why don't you sit down. So things are actually all right.

Hambone: Not exactly, Mr. Herman.

Christy: What do you mean? Mom always paid the rent on time.

Father: Christy: One more word from you, and I'll let you have it!

Hambone: Now you can see what the real problem is. It concerns the children. Now, I'm not reproaching you, Mr. Herman. After all, they're not yours.

Father: That's for sure.

Hambone: But the children have been so poorly brought up—there have been just too many complaints about them! At any rate, you can't count on a new building anymore, that is, unless you succeed in disciplining the children. Teach them respect and order. You look like the right man for the job! I'm sure you're strong enough to keep these kids in line.

Father: You can bet your life on that, Mr. Hambone! I've only been married a short time, but I'll produce results. Don't worry about it!

Hambone: Well, I certainly won't worry about it. But I hope you do at least! (*Mother enters.*) Good bye, Mr. Herman. Good bye, Mrs. Herman. (*Exits.*)

Christy: That guy's always after us, the old goon!

Mother: What did he want now?

Father: What did he want? He said that we won't be able to move into one of the new developments. On account of your children. I've always told you that you let the kids run around like wild animals! They always get their own way with you! (*The children cheer about a touchdown on the tv.*) Quiet down, now!

Mother: Now, wait a second....

Father: No, you wait a second. From now on there'll be a new way of doing things here. And if you try to cover up for the kids, then I'll show you who wears the pants in this family. I'm not gonna let them kick me out onto the street just on account of you. You can bet your life on that!

Mother: Cool off, will you! Calm down. Here's your potato chips and beer.

Father: You know what you can do with that—shove it! I'm going to a bar where I can enjoy the game in peace! (*Exits.*)

Christy: Man oh man, he really explodes when he explodes.

Pete: What's wrong with him??

Christy: Bonehead fed him a few lies about us so he gets all steamed up.

Mother: Will you two be quiet! Please!

Christy: Mom, why d'you marry dad if he only yells at us and wants us to wait on him like servants. It was really much nicer before without him.

Mother: Well, I love him. In spite of it all. Anyway it's much easier when a man's around. Besides that, I thought you two needed a father, and I knew that I couldn't pay for the new apartment without some help. You see it's difficult when you're alone, when you're a single woman—everyone saying nasty things behind my back.

You know how it is.

Christy: But now it's even worse. . . . Why don't you stand up and fight for your rights? We can't go on like this.

Mother: Will you just shut up for once! What do you know about life?! (*She goes into the kitchen.*)

Christy: Man, I've had enough of this rotten place! And if mom won't do anything about it, then—then I'm taking off. You coming with me?

Pete: Where to?

Christy: Anywhere. We'll make up our minds after we leave.

Pete: We've got to know where we're going.

Christy: We'll go to the vacant store Mary Lou's father used to own. Nobody's been there for over a year.

Pete: Great idea! Then we can build ourselves a real neat hideout, and we can lock the door so nobody can get in. Then we can do anything we want. I'll get a job and make money. And you can stay at home and cook and wash—no???

Christy: Hey, that's what we're running away from!

Pete: Well, I'll make my own bed for sure. I promise.

Christy: That's better. C'mon. Let's go.

Both: We're taking off, we're taking off, we're taking off.
Yeah, we've had enough
And now we know what we have got to do.
We're taking off.
Our dad, he yells and screams to get his way,
and mom, she won't stand up to him.
We're taking off.
They tell us what we ought to do.
and never ask us what we want to do.
We're taking off, we're taking off, we're gonna split!

Christy: Tomorrow we'll pack some clothes in our school bags and pretend that we're going to school. Then we'll run away.

Christy and Pete: We're taking off, we're taking off, we're gonna split!

INTERMISSION

Note: At the beginning of the second act, the guitarist at the Berlin production began singing "Man oh man, man oh man, let's all work now hand in hand." He then asked the audience to accompany him.

(*Christy and Pete standing with their school bags in front of the house.*)

Christy: C'mon. Let's get going, otherwise Mary Lou will see us! — What's wrong?

Pete: Maybe it'd be better if we went to school...

Christy: Oh, yeah, that'd be real smart! Mrs. Twiddle would ask to see your notebook, and you'd reach into your school bag and pull out your underpants. (*She digs into his school bag and takes out the underpants and hits him over the head with them.*)

Pete: I don't know, Christy...

Christy: What's wrong with you all of a sudden?!

Pete: Running away is dumb!

Christy: What's the matter? You afraid?

Pete: Are you kidding? I'm only thinking about Mom, and...

Christy: Mom! Mom! If mom wants to put up with everything, that's her own fault. Anyway, I've had enough. I'm taking off! (*Exits*)

Pete: But then everything will get even worse! Christy, wait for me. I'm coming.

(*Just at the moment that he wants to follow her, Mary Lou enters.*)

Mary Lou: Hey, where's Christy off to? She just flew by me without saying a word!

Pete: Christy? — Christy? — Oh, Christy, she had to buy another notebook. (*He keeps trying to make his getaway.*)

Mary Lou: A notebook? But the store's over there!

Pete: The store's over there? Really? Oh yeah, you're right, I mean—I meant a book of stamps, at the post office, over there. (*He tries to leave.*)

Mary Lou: Well, c'mon now. We have to rush otherwise we'll be late for school. (*She starts off.*)

Pete: Right, I'm coming. Don't want to be late....(*He wants to slink away.*)

Mary Lou: Hey!

Pete: Yeah, what's wrong?

Mary Lou: This is the way!

Pete: O.K. I'm coming! (*He takes two steps in her direction and then sneaks away again.*)

Mary Lou: Are you daffy? Boy, you guys are real crazy today!

Pete: Yeah, I know. I mean, no. You go on ahead. I've—I've got to—I've to do you know what. Can't hold it in! —See you!

Mary Lou: Man, do what you want! I'm not gonna be late on account of you! (*She exits shaking her head.*)

Pete: Christy, Christy! Wait for me. I'm coming! (*Exits.*)

VIII

Christy and Pete at the Store

Christy: There it is, Pete!

Pete: There's what?

Christy: The store, dummy.

Pete: You sure it's the right one?

Christy: Sure I'm sure. Finally. It took us three hours to find.

Pete: If we had asked someone who lives around here, we wouldn't...

Christy: We would have been caught, and our plans would have been ruined. Do you think someone's inside?

Pete: But you said that....

Christy: Psst!

Pete: But you said it was vacant. Mary Lou's father moved out of here over a year ago.

Christy: I know, but maybe someone's taken it over since then.

Pete (*pushes the door open carefully*): Are you kidding? Nobody's been here for ages. The place is falling apart.

Christy: Yeah, just like I said. The place hasn't been used for over a year. —C'mon, let's clean up.

Pete: Look over here.

Christy: A comic book. So what?

Pete: It's almost brand new. Someone must have been here recently. What if he comes back?!

Christy: Stop being so scared!

Pete: Me scared?

(*Both hear something.*)

Pete: Someone's coming. Quick let's get out of here!

Christy: Too late! Close the door and hide! And don't make a sound!

(*Mary Lou hops with her doll outside.*)

Pete: Do you hear how he walks. I'll bet he's got a wooden leg!

(*Mary Lou enters the store. All three scare the wits out of one another and then laugh.*)

Mary Lou: What are you guys doing here?

Christy: What are you doing here?

Pete: I thought nobody uses this place!

Mary Lou: Yeah, you're right. That's why I come here sometimes. Nobody bothers me here—normally, that is. Hey, how come you guys played hookey from school?

Christy: Because—because we had to move today.

Mary Lou: Move?!

Pete: Move?!

Christy: Yeah, we live here now. Me and Pete.

Pete: Yeah. That's right. Me and her, and I've got to go to work now!

Mary Lou: Work! Children can't work!

Pete (*building himself up*): Why not? Somebody's got to earn the bread around here! (*Exits.*)

Mary Lou: Tell me something, what's wrong with you guys? Have you gone nuts?

Christy: What do you mean? We've run away from home.

Mary Lou: Why d'you do that?

Christy: Why don't you tell me first what you're doing here?

Mary Lou: Why me? This is our store.

Christy: Was your store. Remember, your father moved out. Anyway the place is going to be torn down soon.

Mary Lou: Well, I come here every now and then because, because...

Christy: Well?

Mary Lou: Well, when they fight at home, then I come here with Topsy until it's all over.

Christy: But you always tell me how wonderful it is at your place.

Mary Lou: It *is* wonderful. Now, you tell me why you've run away.

Christy: You just gave the answer.

Mary Lou: I did?

Christy: Because they're fighting at home, because dad's always ordering mom around and yelling at us...

Mary Lou: But that's the way it always is. Fathers are just fathers. You can't change them.

Christy: And so why do you sneak away whenever there's a fight in your house?

Mary Lou: It never lasts long. It only happens because mommy answers daddy back. When I grow up, I'll never speak back to my husband. I'll make sure that he has everything he wants, and then there can be no fights. Besides you're not supposed to run away.

Christy: Bla, bla, bla. I'm not gonna put up with things the way they are anymore. When I grow up, I'm gonna learn to do something I enjoy just like a man, and when I marry, my husband'll do housework sometimes, or me sometimes, and sometimes we'll do it together.

Pete (*comes*): Christy! Christy. I just earned some money.

Christy: What? So fast?

Mary Lou: I don't believe it. You're lying!

Pete: I'm not lying, goatface! Here's a quarter.

Christy: Great! What kind of work are you doing?

Pete: I'm a—a traffic director at the parking lot over there.

Christy: They pay you money for that?

Pete: Of course. It's right next to the shopping center. There aren't many parking spaces, so when cars come, I direct them to a free space. The people are so happy that they give me money. Well, sometimes they do.

Christy: Fantastic! Tomorrow I'll go do it, too.

Pete: Hey, this job's only for men. You go buy something to eat. I've worked hard for the money.

Christy: Hey, wait a second! What'd you say? For men only! I've had enough of that talk: for men only, for women only.

Mary Lou: But, Christy, he's right. Girls are different than boys.

Christy: I'm a girl, but I'm not his maid.

Pete: Man, Christy, I was just putting you on.

Christy: You know we ran away especially because we wanted things to be different, and now you begin doing the same lousy things all over again.

Mary Lou: You always want things different. That's your trouble, Christy. I'm gonna go home now, or else my mommy will worry about me. And you guys better go home, or else the police will come and get you.

Pete: I thought that there was a fight going on at your place?

Mary Lou: I'm sure it's over by now. Mommy's probably made up to daddy, and he'll be nice again.

Christy: Tell me something: you didn't squeal on us in school, did you?

Mary Lou: I'm no tattletale. I didn't even know where you were.

Pete: Good thing you didn't. It'll be all over for you if you tell on us!

Mary Lou: I only said that I met you on the way to school and that Pete didn't want to come with me which seemed pretty strange to me.

Pete and Christy: You did tell on us! You rotten fink!

Mary Lou: Telling the truth is not tattling.

Pete: If you tell people that we're living here, I'll cut out your
tongue!

Mary Lou: I never tattle! (*Runs off.*)

Pete: She's going to tell on us for sure.

Christy: I know.

Pete: We've got to get out of here.

Christy: Let's wait and see. If she really tells, then we just have
to move. Now, let's straighten out this mess here.

Pete: How can we live here without furniture?

Christy: We'll use wooden crates.

Pete: There are none here.

Christy: Well then, we've got to get some.

Pete: Where d'you suggest?

Christy: Guess!

Pete: C'mon tell me.

Christy: In the lot where dad works. I saw a lot of them there.
Most of them were empty, so we won't be stealing them.
Usually they're just thrown away.

Pete: Good! We'll get a few from there, but nobody better see
us. We'll sneak around carefully like Indians. (*He gives
off an Indian war cry.*)

Christy: Hey, you gone mad?! Be quiet. Now, let's go. (*They
exit.*)

IX

Christy and Pete at the Factory Lot

Christy: Here it is!

Pete: There's the crates!

Christy: Hey, look. One of those fork lifts! You think that's
dad's?

Pete: Could be. It looks just like the one he told us about.

Christy: C'mon. Let's get the crates before someone sees us.

Pete: Be careful.
(*They sneak into the middle of the lot where the crates and
fork lift are standing. They reach the car without anyone
seeing them. They now become more daring.*)
Pete: What a great machine! You think it can lift up those
 huge crates over there?
Christy: Sure it can. And they weigh at least a thousand
 pounds.
Pete: It must be a lot of fun to drive one of these cars. (*He
 climbs up on the driver's seat and plays with the levers.*)
Christy: Pete, don't fool around with it, otherwise it'll start up
 and someone will come.
Pete (*makes the sound of a motor*): Rrrrrrrrrr.
Christy: Let me try it.
Pete: Sit down next to me. You can work the levers.
(*Christy climbs up next to him.*)
Pete: Fantastic, huh?
Christy: You really feel strong sitting on top of this baby.
Pete: I'm gonna drive a fork lift too, when I grow up. That'll
 be fantastic. Then I can zoom around the whole day long
 lifting huge crates!
Christy: Every day, morning till night. I bet you'd get tired of
 doing it after awhile.
Pete: Yeah, maybe. One thing's certain: my rear would sure
 hurt. (*Both laugh.*)
Pete: Hey Christy, someone's coming!
Christy: Quick. Hide!
(*They hide themselves. Their father comes with a beer can and
newspaper. He's evidently taking a break.*)
Pete (*whispers*): There's dad! Wow! If he catches us!
Christy: Psst! Be quiet!
(*Father sits down on the fork lift, opens the beer can, and
begins to read the newspaper.*)
Christy: He's going to sit there now!
Pete: He's probably taking a break.
Christy: I hope not too long otherwise we'll be stuck for the
 rest of the day.
Pete: Psst! Someone else is coming.

(*Sneak the foreman enters.*)

Sneak: You got no brains, do you? I told you that we had to assemble two hundred crates before four o'clock. They're gonna pick them up in fifteen minutes.

Father: You told me that just a half an hour ago. I can't do the job that fast.

Sneak: If you would work instead of sitting around here, you could be finished by now, goof-off!

Father: But this is my break.

Sneak: Your break! Do you see me taking a break? Don't give me any of your lip, and get back to work! It's me who's responsible for everything here, and the crates better be ready on time! You think I want the boss yelling at me?!

Father (*grumbles*): If you tell me too late, then it's not my fault.

Sneak (*bellows*): I'm telling you for the last time, no back talk! If you start becoming difficult, I'll make things difficult for you! I hope you get what I mean. Either you get a move on, or you can start looking for a new job! There are a million guys out there who'd jump at having a job like yours. Don't forget that!

Father: Look, Mr. Sneak, I'm not lazy, if that's what you mean. I'm entitled to take a break twice a day. Union rules.

Sneak: You listen to me, Herman. I don't have time to sit around and argue, especially not with *you*! Do what I say, or clear out! And if you clear out, it'll be for good!

Father (*puts down the beer, folds the newspaper*): Don't worry, I'll finish the job.

Sneak: Now you're coming to your senses. If you had done what I asked for in the first place, I wouldn't have had to yell so much.

Voice (*offstage*): Sneak!!!! Sneak!!! Get over here!

Sneak: Right away, boss. (*Sneak exits. Father follows him.*)

Christy: Did you see that?

Pete: Of course I did. You think I slept through all that noise?

Christy: That guy really chewed dad out the way he always chews us out!

Pete: Let's get out of here before he comes back.
Christy: Right. C'mon. Let's take off.
Pete: What about the crates?
Christy: Oh, forget about the crates. C'mon.
(*Both run off.*)

X

(*Christy and Pete return to the store. They are both tired out.
Christy is pondering something.*)
Pete: Dad may have seen us.
Christy: So what?
Pete: Now what's the matter with you? You lost your mind or
something?
Christy: Dad can't even take a break at work. He lets himself
be pushed around like in kindergarten. Why doesn't he do
something about it?
Pete: He can't. They'll fire him if he does. You heard that.
Christy: Well, I don't believe it. I just don't believe it! I'm
positive that dad can do something about it.
Pete: He could take off, maybe. That'd show them!
Christy: That'd show them nothing. He's got to stay there.
He's got to do something so they won't treat him like that.
Pete: Then we shouldn't run away either. It's not right
running away the way we did.
Christy: That's it!! Running away is no answer. It's dumb. It's
got to stop.
Pete: What's got to stop?
Christy: Just pay attention to this:
The boss, he always yells at Sneak.
Then Sneak begins to yell at dad.
And dad then takes it out on mom.
And mom, she yells at us.

Because,
We run away from mom,
And mom, she backs down from dad.
And dad, he backs down from Sneak.
And Sneak, he backs down from the boss.

Christy and Pete:
Because
If you don't fight back, you feel low—man oh man!
So you pick on others to feel big.
It's the same old story, you know,
until someone says: that won't do.

Stand up for yourself,
Stand up, fight for your rights,
and keep on asking things
that make the others think.

Stand up for yourself,
Stand up, fight for your rights,
Stand up for yourself,
Stand up, fight for your rights......

(*As they sing, they march home.*)

XI

In the apartment

(*Mary Lou rings the doorbell.*)
Mother: It's open!
Mary Lou (*hypocritically*): Hi, Mrs. Herman, haven't Pete
    and Christy come home yet?
Mother: Hi. No—I don't even know where they are.
Mary Lou: But I do!

(*Pete and Christy come running outside.*)

Mother: Well, where are they, Mary Lou?

Mary Lou: Well, they weren't in school today. That I can tell you.

Mother: What!?

Mary Lou: You see, it's like this: they wanted—

(*Pete and Christy enter the apartment.*)

Christy: Here we are again!

Pete: We're home!

Mother: I can see that. How come you two weren't in school today?

(*Mary Lou writhes.*)

Pete: We wanted to run away.

Mother: What did you want to do?

Christy: We wanted to run away, for good.

Pete: For a year, maybe.

Christy: Or two months, at least.

Pete: A whole week for sure!

Mother: What's going on here? How come?

Christy: Because of dad! Because he's always so unfair...

Pete: ...and because he always hassles us when he comes home from work!

Christy: Always hassling us period.

Pete: So we wanted to run away.

Mother (*upset*): You really wanted to run away? But, but—come into the kitchen first. We'll make something to eat, and then we can think about something to do. (*She goes into the kitchen with Pete and Christy.*)

Mary Lou: Do you want some help, Mrs. Herman?

Father (*comes into the apartment, goes to the dining room table, throws his jacket furiously on a chair, wants to sit down but then sees that the table isn't set*): Not set yet! Damn it! Six o'clock, and the table's not set yet! Hey Sue, Sue! I'm home!

Mother (*from the kitchen*): And I'm in here!

Mary Lou: Hi, Mr.—

Father: It's six o'clock!

Mother: That's right. It's six on the nose.

Father: So where's my dinner?

(*They all come out of the kitchen and stand silently before him.*)

Father: Why're you all looking so dumb? Where's my dinner? I've got a hard day's day work behind me!

Mother (*to Christy*): Where's my dinner? I've got a hard day's work behind me!

Christy (*to Pete*): Where's my dinner? I've got a hard day's work behind me!

Pete (*turns to Mary Lou*): Where's my dinner?

Mary Lou (*bewildered*): Uh—uh, I'll make dinner if you want?

Father: Is this supposed to be a joke? Some kind of put down, huh? What kind of a way is that to speak to me?

Mother: Your way! —Pete and Christy wanted to run away today because of you.

Father: Run away! Because of me? You're crazy! What the hell for?

Mother (*ironically*): Because you're always so friendly, always so helpful, and never order people around—

Father: Very funny. Now cut the crap! I think I'm going out of my mind! You want to make trouble for me. Well, I've got enough trouble at work. But at least I can still get things done the way I want there. They know I mean business when I say something.

Christy: That's not true and you know it!

Father: You calling me a liar?

Pete: We were there today, in the lot where you work.

Father: So? What were you doing there?

Pete: Looking for crates.

Father: Well, what's that prove?

Christy: We saw how this one guy...

Pete: yelled at you all the time...

Christy: and pushed you around...

Pete: and you didn't do a thing!

Father: O.K. O.K. —I don't want to hear anymore. Shut up!

Christy: You're always ordering us around!

Father: Me? Come off it! Anyway, it's me who's responsible for everything around here.

Pete: That's what this guy said, too, the guy who yelled at you.

Father: If you start becoming difficult, then I'll make things difficult for you. You hear!

Pete: He said that, too.

Father (can't speak because he's so furious): I—I really can't believe it!

Christy: That's something he didn't say.

Mother: If the children want to run away, then I'm going with them.

Mary Lou: I think I'd better be going, too. Bye. (*Exits.*)

Father: And me?

Mother: You can give orders to yourself.

Father: I *am* going out of my mind!

Mother: You're repeating yourself.

Father: Well, what do you want? C'mon tell me!

Mother: We want things changed. We want to live on good terms with each other, and if that doesn't work, then we'll just have to separate.

Father: But, but Sue, you can't do that. Think of the children. (*He tries to save himself with irony.*) So, you think I should change myself.

Mother: You're getting the idea.

Father (believes that he's exaggerating a great deal): So, I'm the tyrant of the family, a terror to the children, and you're all the poor oppressed slaves who suffer because of me.

Mother: That's one way of putting it.

Father (shocked, changes his tactics and pretends to be agreeable): O.K. We'll try it your way. I'll change myself. If that's all there is to it. I'm at your service. Now I understand. (*He breathes a sigh of relief and falls into the easy chair.*) But before we begin, I need a beer. Christy, get me—(*Christy doesn't budge.*) Oh, excuse me! I'll get it for myself. After all, I know where everything is. . . .

(*Exits. They're all astonished. Father returns.*) Hahaha, funny isn't it? Go ahead, laugh yourselves to death! Laughing's the best medicine. What can I do for you? Dust the house? Do the homework? Darn the socks? Cook? Wash the dishes? Hey, where's my apron?

Christy: In the kitchen!

Father: In the kitchen! I should know that. What a jerk I am! Well, let's see what there is to eat. (*Goes into the kitchen.*)

Mother: There's a can of tuna in the cupboard!

Father (*from the kitchen*): Tuna—tuna. Good, I'll eat tuna. Oh, and the dishes haven't been washed yet. I guess daddy will have to do them later. Where the hell's the opener? —There it is. Oww!

Pete: I think the tunafish bit his finger...

Father (*re-appears, sucking his thumb. He has a towel draped over one arm and pretends to set the table as though he were a first class waiter*): May I? Delicious, delicious! A French appetizer. Tuna fish in oil. Would you like some, too. Well then, I have to wash the dishes first and then go shopping. (*Everyone is delighted.*) What're you all so happy about?

Mother: We're happy because you want to wash the dishes.

Father: All right, now! Enough of this crap! You know I was only playing!

Mother: You were only playing?

Christy: Hey, that's really too bad. I wanted to help you.

Pete: Me, too.

Father: You really wanted to help...

Mother: Yes, we could all do it together.

Father: Well, if you really want to help...

Mother: Of course we do!

Father: If you really mean it...

Mother: I'll wash the dishes with Pete...(*She goes with Pete into the kitchen.*)

Father: And I'll go shopping with Christy. Now everything's different. I thought that I'd have to do everything alone. (*Christy hums the melody of "stand up, fight for your rights."*) What's that you're humming?

Christy: Oh, just a song:
Stand up, fight for your rights,

and keep on asking things
that make the others think.
Stand up, fight for your rights. . . .
(*Both exit.*)

XIII

The Lot at the Factory

(*Father comes on stage singing "Stand up, fight for your rights, stand up, fight for your rights." He continues to whistle or hum the tune while examining the fork lift. Then he lies down and begins to repair something.*)

Father: Damned clutch! It's always getting stuck. Da Da dadaaaaaadada. (*Tune of song.*)

Sneak (*comes from behind*): Damn it! You're always poking around in the motor of your car. How about sitting on top of it and doing some work! Because of you, goof-off, we never get a delivery ready on time!

Father: What do you want me to do if this stupid machine is always breaking down?

Sneak: You never find time for work, but you always find time to make up excuses! You're supposed to handle the machine with care and keep it in top shape!

Father: I take good care of this machine!

Sneak: Now don't get tough with me. I can use another language with you, you know. And you know what that means: I'll take some money off your paycheck for destroying factory property.

Father: This thing here's at least twelve years old, so how can you expect it to run like a brand new machine in tip-top shape?

Foreman: Listen, Herman, I don't think you understood me. I'm not gonna stand for these continual breaks you take to repair this car! If you took better care of it, you could prevent all these breakdowns. Now I hope I've finally gotten the message through that thick skull of yours!

Father: Yeah, well I've had enough! I've taken all that I'm gonna take from you, Sneak! You're not gonna yell at me like this anymore without a reason. You've been picking on me too long, Sneak, too long!

Sneak: Take it easy, man. No need to explode...

Father: I'm not done yet! I'm not your flunky, and I'm not gonna let myself be whipped by you like some stupid workhorse. And especially not by such a chicken-livered meathead like you!

Sneak: Now, wait a minute...

Father: I said I wasn't done yet! Me and the other drivers here are gonna make sure that nobody shoves us around during our breaks anymore or yells at us because of these moth-eaten machines here. We'll take our case to the grievance committee. So now you can run to the boss and stuff this down his throat! The workers in the delivery section are not going to put up with anymore of your shennanigans. That's it! You can take off now. I've got some work to do. Shove off!

Sneak: Hey man. Mac. Let's not get everything so twisted. I didn't mean it that way.

Father: But I meant it that way! And since when do you call me Mac. I'll tell you when to call me Mac. Now get out of here. Shove off!

Sneak: Man, I really didn't mean it that way! I can't help it. The boss insists that I keep after you guys! When things go wrong, then he dumps all over me. You should see him! What would you do in my place?

Father: I'd stand up for my rights! Just don't put up with his crap! And one thing I can guarantee you: if you ever get up the nerve to talk back to him, you can count on all of us here to support you. I mean that!

Sneak: O.K. —well then—no harm meant—

Boss (*off-stage*): Sneak! —Sneeeeak!!!

Sneak: Oh-oh, I've got to go....you hear, don't you?...I

apologize about before. I didn't mean to be that way...Well, so long (*Exits.*)

Father: Get a load of that. Old Sneak! He's like a different person now! (*Sings.*)

> Stand up for yourself,
> Stand up, fight for your rights,
> and keep on asking things
> that make the others think.

> Stand up for yourself,
> Stand up, fight for your rights,
> and keep on asking things
> that make the others think.

(*Exits.*)

At Home

Father comes in with a bag of groceries which he puts down on the table. Then he goes into the kitchen and returns wearing an apron. He cleans off the table while singing the melody "stand up, fight for your rights." Then he carries the bag into the kitchen.

(*Mother enters. She's carrying a similar bag of groceries and puts it down on the table.*)

Mother: Mac? Are you already home?

Father (*comes from the kitchen*): I'm here. Man, am I here! You can't imagine how great I feel—I'm flying high! I talked with the other workers today. They had the same troubles with Sneak I had. You know the whole story. Anyway, I really let Sneak have it this time. And I mean really! Let me tell you, it was something! First he looked at me as if I had gone off my rocker. Then he became friendly. I'm telling you. He's like a completely different person!

Mother: Sneak friendly?

Father: Sweet as sugar! I don't know why I ever let him dump on me so long. (*He notices the bag of groceries now that he's come out of the kitchen.*) Hey, that bag of groceries?!

Mother: What's the matter with it?

Father: I could have sworn that I just carried it into the kitchen. (*He goes into the kitchen somewhat puzzled.*)

Mother (*follows him with her bag*): Oh no, you didn't go shopping, too!

(*Christy, Pete, Mary Lou enter with a similar bag of groceries.*)

Christy: Mom! Dad!

Pete: We took care of the shopping.

(*Mother and father appear in the kitchen door with their bags.*)

Mother (*apprehensively*): Don't tell me!!?

Pete: Bread, eggs, milk.

Mother: That's what I bought, too.

Father: Me, too.

Mary Lou: I told you this would happen: shopping is women's work!

Father: What do you mean! All you have to do is to divide the work properly, then you save everyone time. We'll learn how to do that soon enough. So, let's get dinner ready now. (*Goes with mother into the kitchen.*)

Mary Lou: Hey, your father's been acting real strange lately. Real different from my daddy.

Pete: Maybe you like your hothead father better?

Mary Lou: Well, I'm not sure. But is he allowed to do things like this?

(*Doorbell rings.*)

Mary Lou (*looks through the keyhole*): Oh-oh, trouble ahead. It's old Hambone. You see, your father's not allowed!

Pete: You are really dumb sometimes! (*He opens the door.*)

Hambone: Can I speak with your father?

Christy: Yeah, and with our mom, too.

Hambone: But I only want to speak with your father.

Pete: He's cooking.

Hambone: Don't pull my leg.

Christy: We're not dogs. We don't pull anyone's leg.

Hambone: Don't get fresh. Now, I want to speak to your fatner, for once and for all.

(*Father comes out of the kitchen with a chef's hat on in addition to the apron.*)

Pete: Oh, dad, Mr. Hambone insists on speaking to mom.

Hambone: Ridiculous, Mrs. Herman. Oh, excuse me, I mean Mr. Herman...My God, look at you!!!

Father: Do you do your cooking in a tuxdeo, Mr. Hambone?

Hambone: Cook? Has your wife run away from you?

Mary Lou (*negatively*): No, they share all the work now.

Mother (*enters*): What's going on here now, Mr. Hambone?

Hambone: I have to speak to your husband. It concerns the new apartment!

Father: You can discuss that with my wife. I've got some work to do. (*Exits.*)

Hambone: Well then, it concerns the children. (*To the mother.*)

Mother: Then discuss it with the children. I've got some work to do. (*Exits.*)

Pete: Well, what can we do for you?

Christy: We'll be glad to help.

Hambone (*to the children*): Well then, there have been too many complaints recently....Oh, this is ridiculous! For the last time: I want to speak with your father. (*Goes into the kitchen.*)

(*Father comes out with a tray of dishes.*)

Hambone (*following him*): Well then, Mr. Herman. Will you please take off this apron and listen to me. I want to talk to you as the man of the house.

Father (*gives him the tray of dishes*): Hold this for me, will you? Thanks. (*He forms a chain with Christy and Pete. They work together beautifully with Hambone holding the dishes which the father passes to the children who place them on the table.*)

Hambone (*doesn't know what to do*): Well then, this is....well, concerning the new building....

Mary Lou (*admires the teamwork*): Hey, that's real neat! I'll practice that with Topsy at home.

Christy: You'd be better off if you'd practice it with your mom and dad.

Hambone: My God, this place is falling apart. No order. No respect....I can tell you one thing: The new apartment......

Father: You got it for us. I know. That's real nice.

Hambone: You're wrong!

Mother (*enters*): We're not wrong. We did some investigating at the city department of housing.

Father: We know what the law is now: families with children definitely and automatically are guaranteed a new apartment when their building is torn down. Even if they don't have children who are kept in chains the whole day long.

Hambone: Do you believe...

Father: We certainly don't believe you!

Mother: Why don't you give up? You can't swindle us anymore.

Christy: Come here, Mary Lou!

(*The children jump and form a circle around Hambone. As they dance, they sing: "Stand up, fight for your rights."*

Hambone (*furious*): Will you call off your brats! This is horrible! I...I'm warning you...You'll hear from me again, Mr. Herman, Mrs. Merman, I mean, Mr. Mermaid. Do what you...Oh, I give up! (*Exits.*)

Mother (*laughing*): I don't think he knows what he's doing anymore.

Pete: He don't even know who's who?

Father: O.K. Let's go Sue, make dinner!

Mother: What?

Father: Ooops? Let's go, Mac. Make dinner!

Mother: I'll help.

Mary Lou: It's really great here now, you know!

Christy: And you said it'd never work.

Mary Lou: I take it all back. It's really neat. I'm gonna try it at my home, too.

(*Sings.*)

> When I come home
> and daddy yells: get me my food, let's go!
> I'll say no.
> And when mommy screams to me:
> You've got to do what daddy says,
> I'll say no.
>
> I won't do a thing, not I,
> if they don't say the reason why
> Then one day,
>   they'll understand.
> That'll be grand.

Mary Lou and Christy:

> When I grow up
> I'll be much more than just a housewife.
> I'll be free.
> Then no one can
> push me, boss me around, or rule my life.
> I'll be free.

Mary Lou, Christy, Pete:

> No need to brag or boast,
> or think you're better than most.
> We'll all grow
> best if we
> use good sense.

Mother, Father, Mary Lou, Christy, Pete:

> When we all argue
> and disagree, the Hambones show their delight, it gives
> them might.
> But if we unite
> and all agree to work hand in hand, then they lose

their might.
All of us now can see
how things could be!
We'll all grow
best if we
use good sense.

Man oh man, man oh man,
let's all work now hand in hand.
Girls and boys, moms and dads,
We're all the same.

Stand up for yourself.
Stand up, fight for your rights,
and keep on asking things
that make the others think.
Stand up, fight for your rights.

I SLAVE AWAY

WE'RE TAKING OFF

STAND UP, FIGHT FOR YOUR RIGHTS

THE BOSS, HE ALWAYS YELLS AT SNEAK, THEN SNEAK BEGINS TO YELL AT DAD AND

DAD THEN TAKES IT OUT ON MOM, AND MOM, SHE YELLS AT US. WE

RUN AWAY FROM MOM AND MOM SHE BACKS DOWN FROM DAD. AND

DAD HE BACKS DOWN FROM SNEAK AND SNEAK BACKS DOWN FROM THE

BOSS IF YOU DON'T FIGHT BACK, YOU FEEL LOW, MAN OH MAN, SO YOU

PICK ON OTHERS TO FEEL BIG IT'S THE SAME OLD STORY, YOU

KNOW UNTIL SOMEONE SAYS: THAT WON'T DO.

1. STAND UP FOR YOURSELF, STAND UP, FIGHT FOR YOUR RIGHTS AND
2. STAND UP FOR YOURSELF, STAND UP, FIGHT FOR YOUR RIGHTS,

KEEP ON ASKING THINGS THAT MAKE THE   OTHERS THINK
STAND UP FOR YOURSELF, STAND UP, FIGHT FOR YOUR RIGHTS

WHEN WE ALL ARGUE (FINALE)

MARYLOU:
WHEN I COME HOME, AND DADDY YELLS   'GET ME

MY FOOD   LET'S GO." I'LL   SAY NO.   AND WHEN

MOMMY SCREAMS TO ME: YOU'VE GOT TO   DO WHAT DADDY SAYS

I'LL   SAY NO   I WON'T DO A THING, NOT I,   IF

THEY DON'T SAY THE REASON   WHY   THEN ONE DAY

THEY'LL UNDERSTAND   THAT'LL BE   GRAND

MARYLOU & CHRISTY:
WHEN I GROW UP, I'LL BE MUCH MORE   THAN JUST A

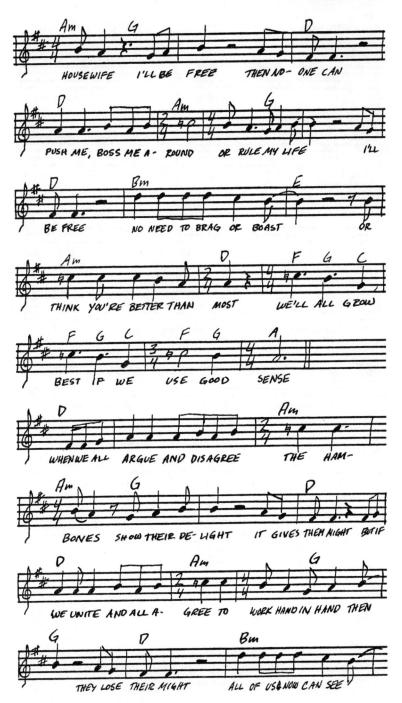

ALL THE SONGS IN "MAN OH MAN" WERE
WRITTEN BY;
WORDS: VOLKER LUDWIG
MUSIC: BIRGER HEYMANN
TRANSLATED FROM ORIGINAL GERMAN: JACK ZIPES
MUSIC ADAPTED: ANNE WARREN

ADDITIONAL BOOKS FROM TELOS PRESS

Marx and Engels on Literature and Art
edited by Lee Baxandall and Stefan Morawski

A comprehensive collection of Marx's and Engels' thought on aesthetics. The detailed Introduction by Stefan Morawski offers the requisite theoretical framework for an enriched understanding of Marxian aesthetics. An excellent introductory text. Bibliography and index are included. 175 pages. Cloth: $6.95. Paper: $2.95

The Mirror of Production
by Jean Baudrillard

Translated with an Introduction by Mark Poster, this work by one of France's most promising young scholars surveys the development of Marxist theory, concluding that the productivist model it generated is not an aberration, but the logical outcome of Marxism's fundamental theoretical flaws. A truly libertarian, emancipatory theory must radically reconsider the whole Marxian tradition and in so doing, Baudrillard provides considerable insight in search of new emancipatory theoretical models. 167 pages. Available in paper only. $2.50

Cultural Creation in Modern Society
by Lucien Goldmann

A collection of Goldmann's best essays. Dealing with a broad spectrum of topics from culture to politics to social organization, these essays provide an invaluable and concise account of Goldmann's position. A lengthy Introduction by William Mayrl places Goldmann and his work in the proper socio-historical context. Approximately 160 pages. Cloth: $6.50. Paper: $3.00

Towards a New Marxism

edited by Bart Grahl and Paul Piccone

A compilation of papers presented at the first **Telos** Conference, held at Waterloo, Ontario, in 1970. The papers represent the acme of the New Left's theoretical development as well as reflecting its inner tensions leading to its eventual demise. Articles by Breines, Buhle, Colletti, Dunayevskaya, Gross, Kosok, Parsons, and Piccone. 240 pages.

Cloth: $8.50. Paper: $2.75

History, Philosophy and Culture in the Young Gramsci

edited by Paul Piccone and Pedro Cavalcanti

This selection of Gramsci's early writings is required reading for all students of Western Marxism. Most selections are drawn from newspapers and magazines: the writings clearly and forcefully convey Gramsci's ideas on the pressing political issues of his day—ideas subsequently developed in much of his later work. The book's five major divisions provide a catalog of Gramsci's thoughts on such topics as the Russian Revolution, World War I, the socialist movement, and other vital issues. 160 pages. Cloth: $6.00. Paper: $2.50

Essays on the New Working Class

by Serge Mallet
edited by Dick Howard and Dean Savage

This anthology of writings is the first work in English to provide a comprehensive view of Mallet's lifework. The three major divisions of the book deal with the "Evolution of the Working Class," "The New Working Class and Technocracy," and the problem of "Workers' Control," particularly as it relates to the May 1968 events in France. A must for anyone interested in the history and structure of the working class in advanced industrial societies. 240 pages. Cloth: $7.00. Paper: $3.50

Order books from **TELOS PRESS**, Sociology Department, Washington University, St. Louis, Missouri 63130, or from your bookseller. Make checks payable to "Telos Press."